William J. Fay

P9-CMT-051

Possessions and the Life of Faith:
A Reading of Luke-Acts

Zacchaeus Studies: New Testament

General Editor: Mary Ann Getty

Possessions and the Life of Faith

A Reading of Luke-Acts

John Gillman

A Michael Glazier Book
THE LITURGICAL PRESS
Collegeville, Minnesota

To my Father and Mother

A Michael Glazier Book published by The Liturgical Press.

Copyright © 1991 by The Order of St. Benedict, Inc., Collegeville, Minnesota. All rights reserved. No part of this book may be reproduced in any form or by any means, electronic or mechanical, including photocopying, recording, taping, or any retrieval system, without the written permission of The Liturgical Press, Collegeville, Minnesota 56321. Printed in the United States of America.

1   2   3   4   5   6   7   8   9

Library of Congress Cataloging-in-Publication Data

Gillman, John.
   Possessions and the life of faith: a reading of Luke-Acts /
John Gillman.
      p.   cm. — (Zacchaeus studies. New Testament)
   "A Michael Glazier book."
   Includes bibliographical references.
   ISBN 0-8146-5675-7
   1. Wealth—Biblical teaching. 2. Bible. N.T. Luke—Criticism,
interpretation, etc. 3. Bible. N.T. Acts—Criticism,
interpretation, etc. I. Title. II. Series.
BS2589.6.W37.G555 1991
241'.68'09015—dc20   91-22660
                                                    CIP

Contents

Editor's Note

Zacchaeus Studies provide concise, readable and relatively inexpensive scholarly studies on particular aspects of scripture and theology. The New Testament section of the series presents studies dealing with focal or debated questions; and the volumes focus on specific texts or particular themes of current interest in biblical interpretation. Specialists have their professional journals and other forums where they discuss matters of mutual concern, exchange ideas and further contemporary trends of research; and some of their work on contemporary biblical research is now made accessible for students and others in *Zacchaeus Studies*.

The authors in this series share their own scholarship in nontechnical language, in the areas of their expertise and interest. These writers stand with the best in current biblical scholarship in the English-speaking world. Since most of them are teachers, they are accustomed to presenting difficult material in comprehensible form without compromising a high level of critical judgment and analysis.

The works of this series are ecumenical in content and purpose and cross credal boundaries. They are designed to augment formal and informal biblical study and discussion. Hopefully they will also serve as texts to enhance and supplement seminary, university and college classes. The series will also aid Bible study groups, adult education and parish religious education classes to develop intelligent, versatile and challenging programs for those they serve.

Mary Ann Getty
New Testament Editor

Introduction

In the early chapters of Luke, when the crowds approach John the Baptist, they raise the question, "What ought we to do?" (3:10). This question is asked again by tax collectors and soldiers (3:12, 14), and later in the Gospel by a rich ruler who addresses Jesus: "Good Teacher, what must I do to share in everlasting life?" (18:18). What are we to do? For Luke this is always a question of salvation, of life or death. The same question is no less pertinent today than it was in Luke's era. Indeed, it presses upon the consciences of all those who read Luke's two-volume work, the Gospel and the Acts of the Apostles.

One important area of life where this question is particularly urgent for believers is that of economics. Some believers with sufficient finances to do so make numerous decisions about money matters, such as buying and selling, borrowing and investing, acquiring and saving. This group is one that enjoys the benefits of goods and services offered by development. To those with plenty, the question is put: What are we to do? Far more numerous are those deprived of any appreciable share in the material resources of society. For this group, worries emerge from a much more fundamental level. Where to acquire enough to eat and drink, where to find a (decent) place to live and raise a family, how to secure employment to make ends meet. To those under the intolerable burden of poverty the question is also raised: What are we to do?

Those who possess much are comparatively few, and those who possess almost nothing are many. Behind the impersonal list of data about those who are rich and those who are poor—two relative classifications to be sure—are, on the one side, lives surrounded by physical comfort, affluence, and sometimes opulence and, on the other side, the trials and struggles, the hopes and aspirations, of suffering people. Many cry out for life's necessities; many desire a more equitable share in the goods of this earth. One current statistical report and one recent symbolic action will serve to bring this into sharper focus. The United States Census Bureau has reported that for 1988, 31.9 million people, or 13.1 percent of the population, fell below the poverty threshold. Commenting on the poverty level in recent years, Isabel Sawhill, an economist at the Urban Institute in Washington has stated: "The poor aren't going anywhere. We're stuck with a high level of poverty, and people who said it was a temporary phenomenon are being proven wrong."[1] Bringing the situation of those too poor to secure adequate housing before the public eye is, for example, a thirty-five-year-old juvenile counselor from Cambridge, Massachusetts. For the better part of a month he chose to live in a cardboard box, which he called a "luxury condo." On the outside it read, "Thousands don't have homes this good. . . ."[2] However, "homelessness" is markedly different for those who voluntarily choose it for a brief period of time than for those who have no other option.

An economics of affluence threatens the moral character of the community, whether it be local, national, or global. It enables a population "to ignore others' pain as well as its own."[3] Reflecting on the contemporary face of American Catholicism, John Tracy Ellis comments that one "lesson that has emerged only within the past generation is that for American Catholics of this late twentieth century their new-found affluence poses a threat to their moral fiber. If up to a generation ago Catholics in this country were free from this danger by reason of their quite limited financial standing, it is no longer true, for the United States is

[1] The comment was reported in the *Los Angeles Times,* August 27, 1986, pt. 1, p. 15. The statistics are taken from *Money Income and Poverty Status in the United States: 1988,* U.S. Department of Commerce, Bureau of the Census, p. 12. The poverty level in 1988 was fixed at $12,092 for a four-person family. The percent of the population in poverty from 1980–88 has been significantly higher than that during the previous period of 1974–79.

[2] See the *Boston Globe,* July 22, 1986, p. 16.

[3] John C. Haughey, *The Holy Use of Money* (New York: Doubleday, 1986), p. 5.

today teeming with Catholic millionaires.''⁴ American Catholics, particularly those whose forebears came from Europe and made up the early immigrant Church in this country, have now established themselves as significant players in the political arena and as affluent participants in economic prosperity. The threat to a person's moral fiber emerges as possessions become the source of one's well being and as one's conscience becomes callous to the material needs of the impoverished. As a result, the evangelical call to realign values, to change one's heart in accordance with the gospel, is neither heard nor heeded.

That personal, community, and national decisions about economic life have a moral dimension has been made clearly evident in the recent pastoral by the U.S. Catholic bishops, "Economic Justice for All: Catholic Social Teaching and the U.S. Economy.'' Faith cannot be separated from everyday life; rather, it is relevant to our decisions as consumers, citizens, workers, and owners. "Economic life," the bishops comment, "is one of the chief areas where we live out our faith, love our neighbor, confront temptation, fulfill God's creative design and achieve our holiness."⁵ As believers we are called "to work actively for social and economic justice" (par. 8). The formation of a Christian vision on economic life has as its foundation the testimony of the Scriptures. The word of God offers a powerful witness of the Creator, of the purpose of creation, and of the dignity of all people. Specifically, the Bible contains many passages that speak directly about economic life.

The need to listen to the biblical witness today is more urgent than ever, for as one author has recently put it, "Money talks all the day long while faith is silent."⁶ A faith that has become accommodated to the prevailing cultural and economic values "cannot speak to money since money has taught it what to say, which is not much, and what not to say, which is to be quiet and learn what 'reality' is."⁷ An open, careful, reflective, and prayerful reading of Luke's two-volume work, the Gospel and Acts, can

⁴John Tracy Ellis, "Lessons from History for the Catholic Church in the United States," *Critic* 40 (1985) 29–40, 37.

⁵"Economic Justice for All: Catholic Social Teaching and the U.S. Economy," *Origins*, vol. 16, no. 24 (1986) 410–455, par. 6.

⁶Haughey, *Money*, 1.

⁷Ibid., 6.

help to reawaken the voice of faith so that its power to speak can be rediscovered. Luke announces to his community, which probably includes at least some several wealthy members, who Jesus is and what faith in Jesus entails when applied to the economic culture contemporary with him. Luke saw that the faith of some of his contemporaries was not allowed to influence their dealings with financial matters and material needs. Hence, Luke retells the Jesus story by putting money matters, material possessions, and the underlying attitudes accompanying both into a faith perspective.

When the modern reader encounters the biblical text, two worlds intersect, that of first-century Christianity and that of modern consciousness. The word of God from the ancient text addresses the contemporary reader such that insight of faith is gained about contemporary problems and meaning is acquired about one's life before God lived out in the community.

This book is intended to be a guide to the Third Gospel and Acts from the perspective of the theme of possessions. In chapter 1, we will discuss the literary features of these writings, including the unity of Luke's two-volume work, the sources used, and illustrations taken from the world of finance. Also, three approaches to the study of possessions will be presented. Chapter 2 focuses on the privileged place of the poor in the Gospel narrative, and chapter 3 discusses the theme of discipleship as this relates to possessions. The final chapter treats the use of possessions in the story of the early Church.

1

Approaches to the Study of Possessions in Luke-Acts

In recent years no lack of scholarly attention has been given to the related themes of the rich and the poor, of material possessions (their use and dangers), and of voluntary poverty in the two-volume work of Luke-Acts. Most commentators now agree that Luke presents a variety of approaches to these themes, rather than one perspective which he imposes upon the Christian community of his day. For example, a number of passages call the would-be disciples of Jesus to renounce all their possessions as a condition of discipleship. Other texts call the believing community to give alms, and still others to share their resources in common. Clearly, a believer cannot follow all these ways at the same time. Once a person has given away all that he or she has, then it is no longer possible to give alms. Nonetheless, a gospel mandate is addressed to all believers to respond in some way to share their possessions according to the purpose of the God who calls them.

Before going to the sacred writings themselves, it is helpful to consider the variety of approaches that biblical commentators have used in studying this theme. Hence, in this chapter we will first take a brief look at the literary features of Luke-Acts and then present three different approaches, or interpretative "windows," through which commentators are trying to understand what Luke has to say about possessions. These are the sociohistorical-redactional approach, the cultural-anthropological approach, and the literary-symbolic approach.

A. *Literary Features of Luke-Acts*

1. *Literary Unity of Luke-Acts.* When the New Testament canon was assembled, the Gospel of Luke and the Acts of the Apostles were separated from each other by the Fourth Gospel. Unfortunately, this physical arrangement of the texts can hinder the reader from recognizing the overall unity of Luke's writings. The introductions to both Lukan writings are addressed to the same figure, one called Theophilus. The Gospel is, in Luke's words, "an orderly account for you, most excellent Theophilus, that you may know the truth concerning the things of which you have been informed" (1:3-4). The first words of Acts, part two of Luke's literary work, make a direct link with part one: "In the first book, O Theophilus, I have dealt with all that Jesus began to do and teach, did and taught, until the day when he was taken up" (1:1). Luke tells as one story about how God fulfills his promises to Israel, first in the life, death, and resurrection of Jesus, and then in the birth and growth of the early Church. In Luke's single vision, "what happens with Jesus foreshadows the church's experience and what happens in the church finds meaning as the continuation of Jesus' story."[1] By showing how God does indeed fulfill his promises in this way, Luke provides for Theophilus and the rest of the Christian community "certainty" about "the events that have been fulfilled among us" (Luke 1:1).

As an author Luke writes from three perspectives: as a theologian, a historian, and a biographer. As a theologian he is concerned to show how God's plan is fulfilled and hence brings salvation to all, especially now to the Gentiles. As a historian he uses sources, both literary and oral, to demonstrate that this new Christian movement has its legitimate place on the stage of world events. As a biographer he tells in theological language the story of his main characters, that of Jesus in the Gospel, and that of Peter and Paul in Acts. Luke accomplishes all of this with remarkable skill in a single narrative.

---

[1]Luke T. Johnson, *The Writings of the New Testament: An Interpretation* (Philadelphia: Fortress, 1986) 199.

Taking seriously the narrative unity of Luke's work, the literary critic urges the reader to consider the individual texts, for example, those on possessions, not as isolated passages but as integral parts of the total narrative fabric. Read from this perspective, one should note carefully how each part fits into the immediate narrative context and into the whole. The repetition of themes and their variations are to be observed. One significant recurrent theme is the reversal of fortunes. First proclaimed in Mary's canticle at the beginning of the Gospel (1:51-52), this theme is echoed throughout the text, for example, in the Beatitudes/woes regarding the poor and the rich (6:20, 24) and very dramatically in the story of the rich man and Lazarus (16:19-31). Literary signals such as key words and phrases serve as clues to discern connections in the story between episodes, whether juxtaposed or separated by several chapters. For instance, the recurrent question "What are we to do?" is not an isolated query from the curious but for Luke a crucial concern leading to salvation or damnation. Our approach to the study of the material on possessions will follow for the most part this literary method, that is, reading the text in its final form handed down to us as a unified, coherent narrative.[2]

2. *Sources Used by Luke.* Other approaches to the Gospel and Acts concentrate upon the sources used by Luke (source criticism) and the way in which Luke creatively uses or edits these sources in the narrative he writes (redaction criticism). What are the sources Luke had available? At the beginning of the Gospel prologue he refers to others before him who "have undertaken to compile a narrative of the things which have been accomplished among us" (1:1). Many, though by no means all, commentators take the position that Luke used the Gospel of Mark and a hypothetical source called simply "Q" (from the German *Quelle,* which means source). The Q source does not exist as such today, but is reconstructed from the Gospel material common to Matthew and Luke that is not found in Mark. This "source" con-

---

[2]For recent authors who use this method, see Robert C. Tannehill, *The Narrative Unity of Luke-Acts: A Literary Interpretation,* Vol. 1 (Philadelphia: Fortress, 1986); Charles H. Talbert, *Reading Luke* (New York: Crossroad, 1982); idem, *Acts* (Atlanta: John Knox, 1984); and Robert F. O'Toole, *The Literary Unity of Luke's Theology,* Good News Studies 9 (Wilmington: Michael Glazier, 1984).

sists of many sayings of Jesus; it lacks a passion narrative. In addition to these two sources, Mark and Q, many posit a third source used by Luke, usually abbreviated L (Lukan) or S (from *Sondergut,* meaning special material), which contains Gospel material found only in Luke; for example, the parable of the Prodigal Son (15:11-32) and the narrative of Jesus as a guest at Simon's house (7:36-50).

From a source-critical perspective, the material in Luke's Gospel on possessions can be differentiated without too much guesswork as deriving from Mark, Q, or the special Lukan material.[3] Luke has taken over from Mark a number of passages dealing with possessions and, in some instances, has radicalized Jesus' mandate. Mark's account of the call of the disciples (Mark 1:16-20) has influenced Luke's episode. In the initial call story from Mark the first four disciples, Simon and Andrew, James and John, leave their *nets* to follow Jesus; in Luke they leave *everything* to follow him (5:11; cf. Mark 1:18, 20). The same intensification occurs in the call story of Levi, who leaves *everything* to follow Jesus (5:28; cf. Mark 2:14). In the instruction to the Twelve in chapter 9, Luke retains the theme of taking little or nothing with them on the journey (9:1-6; cf. Mark 6:7-13), and applies this to the seventy in chapter 10 (vv. 3-4). Luke also records the saying about gaining the whole world and losing one's self (9:25; cf. Mark 8:36). From Mark's Gospel, Luke takes the story of the rich man who is asked to sell what he has and give to the poor (18:18-30; cf. Mark 10:17-31). Luke accentuates the command: "Sell *all.*" Included by both Mark and Luke in this passage is the saying from Jesus about it being easier for a camel to go through a needle's eye than for a rich man to enter the kingdom of heaven. Like Mark, Luke also has the passages about giving to Caesar those things that are Caesar's (20:20-26; cf. Mark 17:13-19); the condemnation of the scribes, who devour widows' houses (20:45-47; cf. Mark 12:38-40); and the poor widow whom Jesus observes giving all she has to live on to the treasury (21:1-4; cf. Mark 12:41-44). Jesus' explanation of the seed sown among thorns as being choked off by the "delight in riches" in Mark is taken up

[3] For a brief discussion of Luke's use of traditional material on possessions, see Joseph A. Fitzmyer, *The Gospel According to Luke,* Anchor Bible, Vols. 28 and 28a (Garden City, N.Y.: Doubleday, 1981, 1985), Vol. 28 247-248. (Subsequent references to vols. 28 and 28a will be indicated by "I" and "II" respectively).

and radicalized by Luke: Riches themselves stifle the seed (8:14; cf. Mark 4:19).

From the Q source Luke takes over four beatitudes, including "Blessed are the poor" (Matthew has "in spirit"), and perhaps the four woes, beginning with "Woe to you rich, for your consolation is now" (6:20, 24; cf. Matt 5:3). This source also provides Luke with the sayings about giving one's coat as well as one's shirt (6:29; cf. Matt 5:40); giving "to *everyone* who begs from you" (6:30; cf. Matt 5:42a, which has "give to *him* who begs from you"); lending without expecting repayment (6:34, 35; cf. Matt 5:42); "give and gifts will be given to you" (6:38; cf. Matt 7:2); not being anxious about food and clothing for the body (12:22-31; cf. Matt 6:25-33); the Son of Man having no place to lay his head (9:58; cf. Matt 8:20); and not being a slave to two masters, God and mammon (16:13; cf. 6:24). From the parable tradition of Q, Luke tells the story about the sums of money given out to be invested (19:11-27; cf. Matt 25:14-30). This evidence indicates that Luke not only preserves most of the material about renouncing wealth from his sources, Mark and Q, but in many instances also accentuates it.

Beyond this, there is a considerable amount of material on possessions that is unique to Luke. In Mary's canticle Luke announces a reversal of fortunes for the proud, the mighty, and the rich on the one hand and the lowly and the hungry on the other hand (1:51-52). Only Luke tells about John the Baptist's instructions to share one's clothing and food, not to collect more than is due for taxes, and to avoid extortion and blackmail (3:10-14). In Jesus' inaugural sermon, Luke has Jesus announcing "good news to the poor" (4:16-18; cf. 7:21-22). In the travel narrative Luke has Jesus telling the story of the Good Samaritan, with a scene about the proper use of possessions (10:25-35; cf. 34-35); inviting his hearers to give alms (11:41; 14:33); correcting brothers who are divided over (greedy for) their inheritance (12:13-15); and rebuking a rich farmer for acting like a fool (12:16-21). In parables Jesus instructs the banquet host to invite the poor, the crippled, the lame, and the blind, instead of friends (14:16-24); tells about the interaction of a rich master and his dishonest steward (16:1-13); and shows that judgment will come upon those behaving like the rich man who ignores the needs of poor Lazarus (16:19-31). At the conclusion of the travel narrative is the exemplary action of Zacchaeus, a rich tax collector, who gives half his belongings to the poor and repays four times over those he has wronged. Becoming a follower of Jesus, he is a model disciple (19:1-10).

This brief survey of passages from Luke's Gospel sources shows that he appropriates much of his material on possessions from the tradition common to the other evangelists. Frequently, however, in recasting this material into the fabric of his narrative, he accentuates the demands. Furthermore, he adds a considerable body of stories and sayings from his own unique tradition. More than any other evangelist, Luke treats the theme or "problem" of how to deal with one's possessions and the position of the rich and the poor as important concerns for his community.

Turning to Acts, we find the question of sources and their use more difficult to unravel, such that there is no scholarly consensus. The "we section" sea voyages (16:10-18; 20:5-21:18; 27:1-28:16) indicate that Luke may have had a travel narrative available to him, although it is also possible that Luke himself may have composed these passages on the standard convention that sea voyages are narrated in the first person plural. Luke was obviously familiar with a few incidents in the life of the early community at Jerusalem, with activities of the Church in Antioch, and with the missionary travels of Paul. However, he never refers explicitly to Paul's letters. Hence, as an author Luke seems to have even more literary control in Acts than in the Gospel. The theme of possessions, while figuring prominently in the first few chapters of Acts, occurs only incidentally in the latter chapters. Since Acts is the author's own authoritative interpretation of the Third Gospel, we will have to explore how this elucidates his perspective on possessions in the combined two-volume work.

3. *Illustrations and Vocabulary from the World of Exchange and Finance.* As we move from source-critical considerations back to the literary fabric of the text, one notices, as might be expected, the frequency and prominence of illustrations and vocabulary taken from the world of exchange and finance. This demonstrates an important dimension of the symbolic world shared in common by Luke and his community. Aware of their concern with economic matters, only Luke among the evangelists includes, in addition to the texts mentioned above from the special material,

the illustrations of Jesus about the tower builder (14:28-30) and the lost coin (15:8-10). Also, not surprising but worth noting is the extensive scope of distinctively Lukan language relating to economic matters not found in the other Synoptic Gospels. This paragraph and the following contain some Greek terms, translated into English, relating to the world of finance found only in Luke-Acts: sharing (*metadidōmai,* Luke 3:11); distributing (*diadidōmai,* Luke 11:22; 18:22; Acts 4:35); begging (*epaiteō,* Luke 16:3; 18:35); counting (*synpsēphizō,* Acts 19:19); and counting up (*psēphizō,* Luke 14:28), used in a positive or neutral sense. On the negative side Luke talks about blackmailing (*diaseiō,* 3:14); accusing falsely for gain or booty (*sykophanteō,* Luke 3:14; 19:8); booty or spoils (*skyla,* Luke 11:22); misappropriating (*nosphizō* Acts 5:2, 3); and lovers of money (*philargyros,* Luke 16:14). He mentions a crowd frequenting or hanging about the marketplace (*agoraios,* Acts 17:5) and various forms of currency: gold (*chrysion,* Acts 3:6; 20:33); drachmas (*drachmē* [equal to a day's wage], Luke 15:8, 9); minas (*mna* [a mina equals a hundred drachmae], Luke 19:13, 16, 18, 20, 24, 25); and money offerings (*prosphora,* Acts 21:24; 24:17). Luke alone names a purse as a means to carry money (*ballantion,* Luke 10:4; 12:33; 22:35, 36).

In business dealings Luke knows about stewards (*oikonomos,* Luke 12:42; 16:1, 3, 8); stewardship (*oikonomia,* Luke 16:2, 3, 4); drawing up an account (*oikonomeō,* Luke 16:2); owners (*ktētōr,* Acts 4:34); property (*hyparxis,* Acts 2:45); rent (*misthōma,* Acts 28:30); repayment (*antapodoma,* Luke 14:12); cost (*dapanē,* Luke 14:28); spending an additional amount (*prosdapanaō,* Luke 10:35); soldiers' pay (*opsōnion,* Luke 3:14); hired servants (*misthios,* Luke 15:17; 19:21); and debtors (*chreopheiletēs,* Luke 7:41; 16:5). He speaks about becoming rich (*plouteō,* Luke 1:53; 12:21); those who live in luxury (*tryphē,* Luke 7:25); being prosperous (*euporeomai,* Acts 11:29). Luke alone remarks that the widow who contributes to the treasury is *very* poor (*penichros,* Luke 21:2). Added to this word field are texts in which Luke uses a financial term, whereas Matthew and/or Mark do not in the parallel passage, for example, benefactor (*euergetēs,* Luke 22:25); the impersonal expression "it profits" (*lysiteleō,* Luke 17:2); and storeroom (*tameion,* Luke 12:24).[4] Again, to be clear, the above

[4]Luke 12:24 is the only text where *tameion* means "storeroom." The same term is used elsewhere to mean "innermost, hidden, or secret room" (see Matt 6:6; 24:26).

list gives terms that are only found in Luke's writings but not in the other Gospels. In order to grasp the full range of financial terms in Luke-Acts, one would have to include also all those terms Luke uses in common with the other evangelists. This selection of literary data further impresses upon the reader how prominent financial matters were for Luke's community and how pressing an appropriate faith response was for those with some means.

B. Sociohistorical-Redactional Approach

In recent years much attention has been given to the social setting of early Christianity. Even though the Gospels are not primarily intended as descriptions of social situations, they do contain clues that can assist the careful reader in reconstructing a partial, tentative sketch of the social world(s) of the Jesus movement. For this enterprise, methods from the social sciences are used. Combined with this approach is the application of source and redaction criticism to differentiate various "layers" of material in the Gospels. Three layers are generally distinguished: the earliest Jesus tradition, originating from the historical Jesus and his disciples; the subsequent generation of wandering preachers who orally transmitted the Jesus tradition; and the perspective of the evangelist who shapes these traditions into the written Gospel. Drawing upon previous studies, we will present a brief discussion of the social setting for each of these three groups.

1. *Historical Jesus Movement.* In the Roman Empire of the first century C.E. and specifically in the land of Palestine, a significant portion of the population was impoverished.[5] An immense gap existed between the aristocracy and the rest of the population. One author has commented that "the aristocracy continually reminded the others of their superior position, by their conspicuous consumption, their entourages in the cities, their dress and their titles, by offering their clients inferior food and wine at banquets, and even by the fact that the law discriminated posi-

---

[5]For a recent discussion on the rich and poor in the Eastern Mediterranean of the Roman world see, e.g., Philip Francis Esler, *Community and Gospel in Luke-Acts,* SNTS MS 57 (Cambridge: Cambridge University, 1987) 171-179. Esler draws upon earlier studies by such authors as R. MacMullen, J. Gagé, A. H. M. Jones, and S. Dill.

tively in their favor."[6] During this period when Jesus lived, the poor were many and the rich few. The word used in the Gospels for the poor is *ptōchos,* which means someone dependent upon others for support, or a person who is destitute, poverty stricken, or in extreme want.[7] Given the widespread impoverishment in the first century, the recurrent use of the word *ptōchos* in the Gospels may be taken as an accurate reflection of the social situation of the time and not merely as a reference to the spiritual poverty of those who stand humbly before God.[8]

A number of factors led to the impoverishment of large segments of the population in Palestine: (1) Herod the Great had appropriated large stretches of farmland and then sold them to wealthy landowners. This created great numbers of dependent tenant farmers. (2) The burden of taxes levied by the Romans and by the Herodian dynasty was crushing. Richard Horsley and John Hanson have estimated that the tax from agricultural products paid to Rome and to the Temple treasury probably amounted to over 40 percent.[9] (3) Many small independent farmers, craftsmen, and the urban plebs of Jerusalem fell heavily into debt as a result of high taxes, poor harvests, and famines.[10] As a result, the lenders, usually the aristocracy in Jerusalem, became richer. Their increased wealth was reinvested in additional land or loans (see Luke 6:34 on lending with interest); it was not redistributed to assist the poor. Horsley and Hanson comment that "simply by making loans, the wealthy could have their debtors out in the villages producing goods necessary for their more leisurely life style in Jerusalem" (see Luke 16:5-7).[11] As Luke 12:22 implies ("Therefore I tell you, do not be anxious about your life, what you shall eat, nor about your body, what you shall put on"), Jewish

[6]Ibid., 172–173.

[7]For discussion see Friedrich Hauck and Ernst Brammel, *ptōchos, TDNT* 6, 885–915.

[8]Cf. Luise Schottroff and Wolfgang Stegemann, *Jesus and the Hope of the Poor* (New York: Orbis, 1986) 16. Trans. from *Jesus von Nazareth—Hoffnung der Armen* (Stuttgart, 1978).

[9]Richard A. Horsley and John S. Hanson, *Bandits, Prophets, and Messiahs: Popular Movements in the Time of Jesus* (Minneapolis/Chicago/New York: 1985) 55.

[10]Martin Goodman, "The First Jewish Revolt: Social Conflict and the Problem of Debt," *Journal of Jewish Studies* 33 (1982) 417–427, pp. 418–419.

[11]Horsley and Hanson, *Bandits,* 60.

peasants in Jesus' time apparently did worry about what they would eat and wear.

In the Gospels and Acts the poor are the ones who depend completely upon others for alms in the form of food, money, or clothing (Mark 14:7; Luke 16:20; Acts 3:1-10). They are the paupers, like the sick man Lazarus who longs for table scraps (Luke 16:20), the local poor who hang out on the village streets (Luke 14:21), or the itinerant beggars who congregate outside the villages (Luke 14:23). Those "poor" who may not be beggars are characterized as belonging to "starving groups a cut above beggary: unemployed day laborers, fugitive slaves, or individuals rendered homeless by economic forces, as for example, small farmers driven into an economic corner by burdensome taxes, crop failures, or debt."[12] In general, the poor are the suffering and oppressed Jewish peasantry.

Turning to the person of Jesus himself, there is very little that is known about his socioeconomic situation. According to the Gospels, he was, like his father, an artisan, a *tektōn,* usually understood to be a carpenter (Mark 6:3). Hence, one can assume that Jesus' family had sufficient means for life's necessities; they were not themselves destitute. If the tradition in Luke about his parents offering two turtledoves at the time of Jesus' presentation is reliable, this would indicate a low economic status.

During his public life there is no indication that Jesus practiced his trade. Instead, he and his disciples relied upon the hospitality of others as a regular means of support (cf. Luke 8:1-3). Among those he called to follow him were four fishermen, Peter and Andrew, James and John, the latter two owning a small business (Mark 1:16-20); a tax collector, Levi/Matthew (Mark 2:13-14); and a zealot, Simon (Mark 3:18; Luke 6:15). After their call, these first followers left family, business, and means of livelihood; they shared the lifestyle of Jesus, who had no permanent residence or place to lay his head (Luke 9:58). They became poor by deliberate choice and thereby brought themselves into close identification with the impoverished condition of the poor. They did this to follow the one who proclaimed God's kingdom, God's reign among the people.

---

[12]Schottroff and Stegemann, *Hope,* 16.

Among those Jesus and his disciples associated with were tax collectors, sinners, prostitutes, beggars, the poor, and the sick.[13] Chief tax collectors were in a position to become rich, as was Zacchaeus (19:2). In general, tax collectors were held in contempt and were known for their misconduct. They were often attacked by tradespeople, condemned by the educated and some high-ranking officials, and treated indifferently by those who had nothing on which duties could be levied. Sinners during the time of Jesus were those who practiced despised trades or who were guilty of criminal action. Prostitutes were adulteresses, slaves, or those who sold themselves for economic reasons. The poor, as discussed above, were the destitute, the beggars, or those who had lost their means of livelihood. They were the sick (cf. Luke 14:21, 23; 4:18-19; 7:22), the naked (cf. Luke 3:11; Matt 25:36), and the hungry (cf. Luke 3:11; Matt 6:25; 25:35-36).

What was Jesus' message to the poor? Though our sources make it difficult to recover the actual words of Jesus with any degree of certainty, we can speak of traditions that probably go back to his time. According to Schottroff and Stegemann, Jesus promised the eschatological reversal of fortunes for the rich and the poor.[14] This was a central theme to his preaching and is expressed in such passages as the Canticle of Mary, the Beatitudes, and the parable of the rich person and Lazarus. In the Beatitudes, for example, which many hold originate in some form with Jesus, the poor, the hungry, the weeping, are told that God is already at work establishing the kingdom, and that this kingdom will be theirs. Then, they will laugh, they will be satisfied, they will be full of joy. God will put an end to the wretched conditions of the poor, while the rich will have taken away whatever consolations they now enjoy. Also, the repeated occurrence of the saying "The last will be first, and the first last" (Mark 10:31; Matt 19:30; 20:16; Luke 13:30), which now appears in diverse contexts in the Gospels, originally may have meant that "those who are last now will be first in the kingdom of God, and those who are powerful now and first in society will have lowly places in the kingdom of God."[15]

[13]For discussion, see Schottroff and Stegemann, *Hope,* 6–17.

[14]Ibid., 17–32.

[15]Ibid., 25.

To say it in a word, what Jesus offered the poor is hope. He identified with their plight, promised them a reversal of their social destiny, and proclaimed to them the good news of God's reign. Although others were not excluded, it was the poor who were the primary recipients of God's reign of justice, love, and peace.

2. *Wandering Prophets.* Beginning with the historical Jesus and extending into the next generation were those known as wandering prophets. By combining a close analysis of the sayings source (Q) with what is known about social uprootedness in the middle of the first century C.E., commentators have sought to identify the teachings and social situation of this group.

The tradition of the wandering prophets begins with Jesus himself. He is presented by Luke as a prophet like Moses (see e.g., Acts 3:22; cf. Deut 18:15). He is "the eschatological traveler who crisscrosses the land, making sure that everyone has the opportunity to hear God's gracious invitation" (Luke 4:14, 43-44; Acts 10:38).[16] As an itinerant prophet Jesus receives hospitality from Simon, at whose house Jesus offers salvation to a sinful woman (7:36-50); Jesus heals and teaches in the house of a leading Pharisee (14:1-24). Received into the home of Martha and Mary, Jesus underscores the importance of listening to his words of instruction. According to the wandering prophets who reflected the lifestyle of the itinerant Jesus, the instructions given to the Twelve (9:3) and to the seventy (10:4) to take no provisions with them on the journey but to rely instead on the hospitality of those who receive them are a validation of their own lifelong itinerant ministry.[17] Only someone who has "renounced all that he has" (Luke 14:33) including home and family (18:29) can claim legitimately to be a follower of Jesus.

In the sayings source the poor whom Jesus called were now the disciples and, by application, the wandering prophets. Having very little themselves, they lived with and called others to an unlimited trust in God. To all of Israel they taught freedom from worry and anxiety (Matt 6:25-33 [Q]; Matt 10:28-31 [Q]). To the farmers, the day laborers, the poor, and the slaves, to those anxious

---

[16]John Koenig, *New Testament Hospitality: Partnership with Strangers as Promise and Mission,* Overtures to Biblical Theology 17 (Philadelphia: Fortress, 1985) 93.

[17]Ibid., 94.

about food and clothing, the prophets taught that human life is "more than food and the body more than clothing" (Matt 6:25). The messengers' own lack of equipment—no bag, no supplies, no money, no permanent residence—attested to their absence of anxiety about survival and their radical trust in God. In this way they sought "an alternative to the life of the ordinary people with its oppressive anxiety about daily survival."[18]

The social situation in first-century Palestine, which correlates with the sayings source, has been studied particularly by Gerd Theissen.[19] According to Theissen, the economic and political crises led to "social uprootedness," which took the forms of emigration, banditry, resistance struggles, and vagabond radicalism. Characteristically, this social uprootedness meant breaking familial ties and leaving one's original residence. In this environment of social upheaval, Jesus "called into being a movement of wandering charismatics."[20] Jesus, those he called, and the next generation of wandering prophets gave a religious interpretation to their radical "ethos," which they hoped would be an example to others.[21]

Regarding the rich, the wandering prophets emphasized that they were distant from God, rather than preaching the eschatological reversal of their condition, a central theme from the time of Jesus. Furthermore, they pointed out the enslaving grip that possessions could have over human beings. Thus they warned those rich for whom wealth, rather than the Lord, had become their master (Luke 16:13; cf. Matt 6:24).

---

[18]Schottroff and Stegemann, *Hope*, 47.

[19]Gerd Theissen, *Sociology of Early Palestinian Christianity* (Philadelphia: Fortress, 1978; trans. John Bowden from *Soziologie der Jesusbewegung* [München, 1977]) See also his earlier essays: "Wander-radikalismus: Literatursoziologische Aspekte der Überlieferung von Worten Jesu im Urchristentum," *ZTK* 70 (1973) 245–271; "Itinerant Radicalism: The Tradition of Jesus Sayings from the Perspective of the Sociology of Literature," *Radical Religion* 2 (1975) 84–93; " 'Wir haben alles verlassen' (Mc. X 28): Nachfolge und soziale Entwurzelung in der jüdisch-palestinischen Gesellschaft des. 1. Jahrhunderts n. Ch.," *NovTest* 19 (1977) 161–196.

[20]Theissen, *Sociology*, 8.

[21]For an evaluation of this thesis of Theissen see, e.g., Schottroff and Stegemann, *Hope*, 48–49; and Richard A. Horsley, *Jesus and the Spiral of Violence: Popular Jewish Resistance in Roman Palestine* (San Francisco: Harper & Row, 1987) 228–231. Horsley rejects Theissen's thesis and argues that Jesus' concern was on local community life, not on calling "into being a movement of wandering communities."

3. *Luke's Community.* It is widely accepted by commentators that Luke-Acts is intended for a Gentile Christian audience in a predominantly Gentile setting. Throughout Luke-Acts the author shows that the salvation promised the Jews in the Jewish Scriptures is now extended to the Gentiles. Acts concludes on this theme: "Let it be known to you then that this salvation of God has been sent to the Gentiles; they will listen" (Acts 28:28). While Acts repeatedly shows the Jewish mission to be failing, it is the Gentiles who are receptive.

   a. Upwardly mobile community. The high literary style of Luke-Acts, especially of the prologues, implies that the author himself came from the upper levels of Greco-Roman society. Luke was evidently wealthy enough to have the leisure time to receive a literary education unavailable to most others.[22] Within the text we also find other clues to the social status of this predominantly Gentile community. The first clue is given in the prologue. As we have seen, the prologues to both the Gospel and Acts name as the addressee a person called Theophilus. Although otherwise unknown, the address itself gives us some glimpse of his social status. In antiquity a formal prologue often indicated official publication with the addressee serving as the sponsor or patron of the writer.[23] This implies that Theophilus had sufficient wealth to finance publication. Furthermore, he is called "most excellent" (Luke 1:4; see also Acts 23:26; 24:3; 26:25), a title of honor given to an official suggesting that he "was prominent and socially respected and probably well off, or highly placed in the society to which Luke had access."[24] By addressing Theophilus as "most excellent," the author suggests that he (the author) is in a subordinate position to a person of greater status in the social structure. The high ranking Theophilus was undoubtedly a catechumen or a neophyte (cf. 1:4) who received Luke-Acts not as a private writing but as instructions for other Christian readers of his own day, many of whom were also well off.

   Within Luke's account we meet well-to-do members of the community whose wealth consisted of money, land, or business en-

[22]See Eisler, *Community and Gospel,* 184.

[23]Cf. Johnson, *Writings,* 198.

[24]Fitzmyer, *Luke,* I, 247.

terprises. Among the tax collectors mentioned (3:10-14; 19:1-9) is Zacchaeus, the chief tax collector, who is described as a "wealthy man" (19:2). In welcoming Jesus he receives salvation (19:9). Within the early Christian community there were property holders (Acts 2:45; 4:34). One of these was Barnabas, who owned a farm, sold it, and gave the proceeds to the apostles (Acts 4:37). While not necessarily wealthy, there were also homeowners (Luke 10:38-42; Acts 2:46; 4:34), some whose homes were large enough to host the group of believers. A group of women, including Joanna, the wife of a high-ranking official, had the means to support the Jesus movement (Luke 8:1-3, a text unique to Luke); Lydia, a business woman who dealt in purple goods, hosted Paul and the believers at Philippi in her home (Acts 16:14-15, 40). Luke also counts among those who confessed the Christian faith the centurion Cornelius and his household (11:14); the proconsular governor Sergius Paulus, whose family, according to archaeological speculation, had extensive holdings in Pisidia (Acts 13:4-12); influential Greek women and men from Beroea (Acts 17:12); Dionysius, a member of the court of the Areopagus (Acts 17:34); and the synagogue leader Crispus along with his whole household (Acts 18:8).[25] These business people and officials, some high ranking, indicate that prosperous men and women joined the community and had the means to serve as patrons.

Besides reflecting the socioeconomic makeup of at least a segment of the community, the mention of these well-off people is related to one of Luke's apologetic purposes. He is interested in showing that the Jesus movement was growing in status among the socioeconomic elite. Besides those mentioned above who joined the community, among the ruling elite who gave the gospel and its messengers a favorable hearing were such individuals as the Ethiopian eunuch (Acts 8:26-39), Manaen, "a member of the court of Herod the tetrarch" (Acts 13:1), and some Greek Asiarchs who were friends of Paul (Acts 19:31). The Lukan community was not only recognized but also accepted and joined by influential political individuals and wealthy people together with

---

[25]Like the other Synoptics, Luke also has Joseph of Arimathea, a member of the Sanhedrin, bury the body of Jesus (Luke 23:50-51), although only Matthew describes him as a "rich man" (27:57). Such a description would have heightened his paradigmatic function in Luke's Gospel.

their households. These individuals were "early heroes of the faith" for the community of Luke's own day, many of whom must have had a similar, perhaps somewhat inferior, position in society.[26] From this impressive list of well-placed people mentioned in the narrative, it can be assumed that there were many prosperous members in Luke's community for whom these "heroes" played an exemplary role. Using a contemporary expression, some authors have described the community as "upwardly mobile."

b. Hellenistic social morality and the problem of wealth. Luke attributes to his readers a Hellenistic social morality. They were more likely to invite friends, relatives, or wealthy neighbors to dinner than they were to reach out to disabled street people who could not repay them (14:12-14). They would make loans at interest (6:34). They would measure greatness as benefactors do by exercising authority over others (22:25). Charity or almsgiving for the poor and destitute who could not offer anything in return was virtually unknown.[27] As Louis Countryman comments, in Greco-Roman society "the claim on the giver consisted not in need, but in some pre-existing personal relationship."[28] In response for giving to the poor, the benefactor expected in return titles of honor, inscriptions, statues, and other privileges. Some reciprocity from the person benefited was expected.

Clearly for Luke the wealth of some of the believers as well as of potential converts is problematic. Luke frequently criticizes not riches in themselves but riches inasmuch as they are an obstacle to full conversion and faithful discipleship. Among some of the well-to-do, their progress in assimilating the word of God was stifled by their riches, and hence "they do not mature" (8:14). One of the sharpest critiques of the insular and nonresponsive life of the wealthy is found in the parable of the rich man and Lazarus (16:19-31). The rich man delights in feasting splendidly but is blind to the life-sustaining needs of Lazarus. The parable

[26]See Eisler, *Community and Gospel,* 184.

[27]See John E. Stambaugh and David L. Balch, *The New Testament in Its Social Environment* (Philadelphia: Westminster, 1986) 64.

[28]Louis W. Countryman, *The Rich Christian in the Church of the Early Empire: Contradictions and Accommodations.* Texts and Studies in Religion 7 (New York/Toronto: Edwin Mellen, 1980) 105.

of the rich fool (12:16-21) is a harsh rebuke of those people who sought security for their life by piling up wealth for themselves. Obviously, Luke "is not satisfied with what he has seen of the Christian use of wealth in his ecclesial community."[29]

Reflected also in Luke's accounts is the hesitation some well-placed Hellenistic potential converts felt in joining the community. They were undoubtedly afraid of what this might cost them socially and economically. We have already seen how the Way attracted some high-ranking and wealthy followers, but there were others whose possessions were obstacles. Some considered their business more important than the invitation to the banquet of God (14:16-24 [Q]). Another time we hear that a "very rich" member of the ruling class heard but did not heed Jesus' call: "Sell all you have and give to the poor" (18:22). Only Luke calls this person a ruler, thereby enhancing his social and economic status in light of the elevated status of his readers. Ananias and Sapphira sold their property but were unwilling to acknowledge that they kept some of the proceeds for themselves (Acts 5:1-11). When the wealthy considered joining the community, a number of them were unwilling to share their possessions generously with the poor.

c. The poor. Apart from the upper class, there were the more numerous impoverished members of the lower class. These were the peasants, those with neither property nor special skills, those who did have to worry about what to eat and where to find shelter. Like the passages about wealth, much of the material about the poor in the Gospel comes from the traditions before Luke and reflects the socioeconomic conditions in Palestine from Herod the Great until the aftermath of the Roman-Jewish War of 66–70 C.E. In preserving these traditions Luke's interests are more than historical. He intends to show that God's favor rests particularly upon those who are poor in a material sense. This is as true for his own community as it was at the time of Jesus.

While less is known about the specific causes of poverty and the faces of the poor in Luke's own community, his consistent emphasis on the privileged place of the poor shows that they were very much present within and without the community for which he wrote Luke-Acts.

---

[29]Fitzmyer, *Luke*, I, 247.

d. Itinerant and resident prophets. Were there at Luke's time itinerant prophets who had left all their possessions behind? Undoubtedly there were, but how influential or prominent they were is difficult to determine. As we have seen above, Theissen has argued that "wandering charismatics" themselves influenced the shape of the "sayings source" (Q) material included by Luke as a way of validating their own itinerant way of life.[30] Koenig speculates that Luke himself may have "spent some time in their company."[31] By preserving these traditions, Luke suggests that the way of the wandering prophet was an authentic and rather lasting phenomenon.

Besides the tradition of the wandering prophets, there was another complementary if not competing tradition, that of resident prophets who belonged to a particular local community. This tradition is found mainly in Acts, where Luke is writing most freely (Acts 2:1-4; 11:27-30; 13:1-3; 15:32-35; 19:1-7; 21:8-9; 21:10). Noting that in Acts there is little evidence of the convictions and views advocated by the wandering prophets, Theissen concludes that Luke "fought in his own time the descendants of the first itinerant charismatics who were from his point of view false prophets."[32] However, to find in Luke such a sharp polemic is to overstate the case. More accurate is Koenig's evaluation that "Luke's composition is aimed at building up local leadership so that it can strengthen the whole church *for partnership with the wandering prophets.*"[33]

These two models of wandering prophets on the one hand and resident prophets on the other hand are each associated with distinctive ways of dealing with possessions. Texts about itinerants espouse the idea of giving away all one's possessions and relying upon the hospitality of others; texts about residential leaders presuppose that one has a home to live in and resources to host the local community and to provide hospitality for traveling missionaries.

---

[30]See above, p. 23. According to Theissen, Luke intentionally revokes the radical call for complete renunciation of possessions (cf. 22:35-38) in order to argue against the ethos of the itinerant prophets.

[31]Koenig, *Hospitality*, 94.

[32]Theissen, "Itinerant Radicalism," 91.

[33]Koenig, *Hospitality*, 19 (his emphasis).

C. Cultural-Anthropological Approach

The social structures, commonly shared values, and systems of meaning for the first-century Mediterranean world differ markedly from those of twentieth-century persons. For that reason one cannot expect to understand automatically what the biblical texts and terms mean without giving serious attention to the social systems of the biblical world. The relevant discipline is anthropology, an area of study that seeks to understand cross-culturally the social structures, the common values realized by social structures, and the worlds of meaning in social groups. One author who has contributed significantly to this approach to the biblical tradition is Bruce Malina.

Malina distinguishes four basic social institutions or structures: kinship, economics, politics, and religion. Briefly explained, "kinship is about naturing and nurturing people; it forms the structure of human belonging. Economics is about provisioning a group of people; it forms a society's structure for adapting to a given environment. Politics looks to effective collective action and forms the vertical organizational structure of a society. Finally, religion deals with the overarching order of existence, that is, with ultimate meaning; it provides reasons for what exists and the ways of understanding that develop those reasons."[34] Whereas in the United States the primary social arrangement is economic, in the world of biblical literature it consists of kinship and politics, which are about belonging and power. In Mediterranean antiquity, economics (and religion) were embedded in kinship and polity. An embedded economy "means that economic goals, roles, production, hiring, firing, planning, and the like, are determined by kinship or political considerations, either alone or primarily, and not purely or primarily on the basis of 'economic' considerations."[35]

To arrive at a meaning for the terms "rich" and "poor" from a cultural-anthropological perspective, it is necessary to consider the linguistic company they keep in the narrative. In Luke, "poor" is used with terms naming those imprisoned, blind, and debt rid-

[34]Bruce Malina, "Wealth and Poverty in the New Testament and Its World," *Interpretation* 41 (1987) 354–367, 358.

[35]Bruce Malina, "Interpreting the Bible with Anthropology: The Case of the Poor and the Rich," *Listening* 21 (1986) 148–159, 154.

den (4:18) and the maimed, the lame, and the blind (14:13-21). Luke also calls a woman poor because she is a widow (21:2-3) and Lazarus poor because he is a beggar covered with sores (16:20-22). From this Malina concludes that the "poor" rank "among those who cannot maintain their inherited status due to circumstances that befall them and their family, such as debt, being in a foreign land, sickness, death (widow), or some personal physical accident."[36] Hence, most people then would view the poor not as a permanent social class but a sort of "revolving class" of people. The "poor" refers to those people who have fallen into misfortune.

An understanding of "rich" and its equivalents can be attained by a similar process. The "rich" are those who have an abundance of resources from which they can make offerings (21:1-4); they are the "mighty, proud," the opposite of the "hungry" (1:51-53); they are already consoled and have their fill (6:24-25). In parables the rich man is variously presented as covetous or greedy (12:16-21); as a well-satisfied man with a family of several brothers, unaware of "poor" Lazarus in his presence, who is without family (16:19-31). In a context on greed the Pharisees are called "lovers of money" (16:14), and finally, Zacchaeus, a rich tax collector, is presented as one who takes from the poor and defrauds.

From these and other biblical and nonbiblical texts, Malina deduces three cultural norms that were shared in the first-century Mediterranean world.[37] (1) All goods were limited. There was a finite quantity of goods, and they were in short supply. This meant that a person or group could increase his or her own supply of goods or economic value only at the expense of others. (2) When it came to the necessities of life, no one was destitute. In other words, those things needed for human subsistence were ready at hand. With that as a "given," there was no need to be anxious about food or clothing (Matt 6:25-32). The exceptions were times of drought, famine, or war, when most of the population would lack the basic necessities. (3) The rich person was perceived as inherently evil. It was commonly understood that the rich were

---

[36]Malina, "Wealth and Poverty," 356.

[37]See Malina, "Interpreting," 155; idem, "Wealth and Poverty," 361-366.

either unjust or the heirs of unjust people. The reason supporting this assessment was the perception of limited goods. For a
person to accumulate wealth meant that another or others would
have less.

The true meaning of wealth in the ancient world lay in its use
to provide for the needs of human living, to provide a contented
way of life. Jesus' injunction about giving one's possessions to
the poor was "not about self-impoverishment but about redistri-
bution of wealth; and motives for giving to the poor are not rooted
in self-satisfying charity but in God-ordained, socially required
restitution."[38]

This cultural-anthropological analysis of the biblical texts
challenges at least some of the generally accepted interpretations
of poverty and wealth in Luke-Acts. Two of these are (1) the assumption that there was a group, designated by *ptōchoi,* who were
destitute, without the basic necessities of life; and (2) the conviction that the biblical texts warn about the *dangers* of wealth. The
first assumption is challenged by the contention that everyone
actually had, according to Malina, the necessities of life. The second conclusion is inadequate if one accepts that there was a per-
vasive perception that the wealthy were not merely in danger from
their riches but were indeed wicked. While many of Malina's insights are valuable, he gives insufficient attention to the poor as
being economically deprived. In some cases, for example, that
of the poor widow (21:1-4), it is clear that she is poor not only
because she has fallen into misfortune by becoming a widow
(Malina's emphasis) but also because she is economically poor.[39]

D. Literary-Symbolic Approach

In Luke-Acts the language of possessions can be interpreted
not only literally but also symbolically or metaphorically. This
approach has been taken by Luke T. Johnson[40] and is related to

---

[38]Malina, "Wealth and Poverty," 366.

[39]For a response to Malina, see Paul Hollenbach, "Defining Rich and Poor Using Social
Sciences," *Society of Biblical Literature 1987 Seminar Papers* (Atlanta: Scholars Press, 1987)
50–63.

[40]Luke T. Johnson, *The Literary Function of Possessions in Luke-Acts,* SBL Diss. Series
39 (Missoula: Scholars Press, 1977); and *Sharing Possessions: Mandate and Symbol of Faith,*

the literary structure of the narrative. Johnson identifies the dominant pattern in Luke's story as that of "prophet and people." Jesus is God's prophet, like Moses, sent to the people to bring salvation. The people in the narrative are presented as either accepting or rejecting Jesus. Those who reject God's prophet are themselves rejected from among God's people.

According to Johnson, the use of possessions is to be interpreted within the framework of this literary pattern. The manner in which people deal with their possessions expresses symbolically whether they accept or reject God's prophet, for the use of possessions expresses the disposition of the human heart in response to God's visitation among the people.

To appreciate the communication symbolized by the language of possessions, Johnson offers some reflections on "being" and "having," two dimensions of our identity as persons. That which is most central to the person, for example, one's heart, one's head (thus, that we say, "my heart" or "I have a head"), is to be distinguished from more exterior things, for example, "my clothes," "my house," or "my stocks." That which a person "has," for example, one's body, one's possessions, which may be understood as the extension of the body, are symbols of the person's intentions. Just as the human body has the capacity to express the human spirit, so also one's possessions can be symbolic expressions of ourselves. The disposition taken toward one's possessions symbolizes a person's self-disposition.

The Christian who clings to possessions or who identifies life with having abundant material things is in danger of falling into idolatry. Things become idols, served or worshiped by the human spirit that is held in bondage to them. In Luke 12:15-21 the rich man is called a fool not because he is wealthy but because he identifies his life's security with the quantity of possessions he seeks to store up for himself. In 14:16-24 the master of the banquet is angry with his invited guests not because they have possessions but because they choose to cling to them.

The proper attitude toward those "things" that we possess, including our very selves, is to consider them as gifts from God to

Overtures to Biblical Theology (Philadelphia: Fortress, 1981). The former work, of a more technical and exegetical nature, provides the foundation for the theological reflections about possessions in the latter book.

be shared with others. If we consider all that we have and are as a gift, then we will relate to others as gift. This, too, is expressed symbolically, as is done by the Samaritan who shares his medicinal skills and his money with the victim in the ditch (10:25-35). In the story of the father with two sons, after the younger son dissipates his inheritance and thereby diminishes himself, the father bestows on him the family's most precious possessions to celebrate his return (15:11-32). To share one's possessions is to express one's faith in the Creator who creates, sustains, and saves us.

While acknowledging that the Lukan Jesus does not prescribe one clear, concrete mandate for dealing with material things, whether that be complete renunciation, giving alms, offering hospitality, or sharing all things in common, Johnson himself gives special emphasis to almsgiving. For this practice, "having" is the necessary condition for "giving." By sharing one's possessions, a believer acknowledges that his or her own life is a gift, affirms solidarity with the human community, and expresses faith in God.

Also working within a literary analysis of Luke-Acts, is Halvor Moxnes,[41] who goes beyond the work of Johnson and studies the socioeconomic structures which emerge from the narrative for the reader. Moxnes starts with the perplexing description of the Pharisees as "lovers of money" (Luke 16:14). He argues that this often misunderstood epithet is to be explained within the framework of social conflicts and economic relations of Luke's Gospel. Rejecting this negative characterization as valid historically, Moxnes interprets it as a literary motif. In both Jewish and Greek polemics, opponents were often accused of being "money-lovers." The author of the third Gospel uses this *topos* as a way of labeling the Pharisees, who in the Gospel are the main opponents of Jesus and his disciples. On a literary level, the Pharisees are seen as "negative representatives of outsiders to the community" of believers.[42]

According to Moxnes, Johnson did not go far enough when he interpreted the "money-loving" Pharisees within the literary

---

[41]Halvor Moxnes, *The Economy of the Kingdom. Social Conflict and Economic Relations in Luke's Gospel*, Overtures to Biblical Theology, Philadelphia: Fortress, 1988. Moxnes also includes many insights from cultural anthropology.

[42]*Ibid.*, 163.

pattern of acceptance and rejection of Jesus, a pattern exemplified with the acceptance of Jesus by the poor, and the rejection of Jesus by the rich. Since the Pharisees generally rejected Jesus, they are portrayed as rich, as loving money instead of God. Moxnes places Johnson's observation in its broader social context. In the Gospel of Luke the Pharisees are presented as striving to uphold the traditional patterns of society through the enforcement of purity laws (see e.g., 5:29-32; 11:37-41), but in doing so they prevented the basic needs of people from being met. Luke draws a direct connection between the Pharisaic misguided concern for purity laws and their economic exploitation of people (see e.g., 11:39 "Oh you Pharisees! Although you cleanse the outside of the cup and dish, inside you are filled with plunder and evil"). In effect, Jesus directly confronts the social structure dominated by the leadership of the Pharisees.

One of the familiar models from social science used by Moxnes to elucidate Luke's social world is that of the patron-client relation. He sees this model as being particularly helpful in understanding the relations between various groups of the society within Luke's narrative, a society which was hierarchial rather than egalitarian. In descending order of power and status the main groups include: 1) the emperor; 2) the rulers in Palestine and Syria: Roman consuls/procurators and tetrarchs (Herodian "kings"); 3) the high priests and Jerusalem aristocracy, large landowners; 4) the subordinates of 2) and 3); officers and officials, agents in local areas of Palestine; 5) village leaders: rich farmers, synagogue leaders, Pharisees; 6) peasants, "full" members of the village; and 7) village "outsiders": deviants, unclean, sinners, tax collectors, needy.[43] Each of these groups, except the lowest, had the ability to influence the behavior of those below them. A higher ranking individual had the role of patron for lower ranking individuals, the clients.

A patron-client relationship is one marked by inequality of power and status. Examples are those relations between landlord and tenant, ruler and servant, lender and debtor, landowner and day laborer. Ranking above a client, a patron provides scarce (economic) resources and political advantages; a client, in turn, reciprocates with expressions of solidarity and loyalty.

⁴³*Ibid.*, 73.

In contrast to this prevailing social world, the Lukan Jesus espouses what Moxnes calls the "moral economy of the peasant." This assumes a radical break from the patron-client relationship which functions to maintain, even exacerbate the inequalities in society. This "peasant economy" is based on the fundamental value of providing food, clothing and housing for those who have such needs for subsistence. In practice this requires that those with means give without expecting a return on a human level, as would be expected in the patron-client relation. The only patron is the ultimate patron, namely God, who will repay those who act in response to human needs.

Conclusion

The various approaches to possessions in Luke-Acts taken together can bring the reader to new depths of understanding when encountering the text. For any given passage each of the approaches outlined above or a combination of them can be employed.

Our own method will be to consider Luke-Acts as a unified narrative. Individual texts will be reflected upon not as isolated episodes but as integral and functional passages to the total narrative. In respecting the literary unity of the text we will try to be faithful to the narrative as it unfolds, without attempting to coerce the various statements about possessions into a unified system. Throughout our discussion we will draw upon the insights offered by the sociohistorical-redactional, cultural-anthropological, and literary-symbolic approaches as discussed above. Although we have briefly mentioned the sources used by Luke, our focus will not be on isolating these sources (source criticism) or on Luke's creative use of these sources (redaction criticism). From time to time we will compare a Lukan passage with the other Synoptics as a way to appreciate Luke's distinctive approach.

2

The Privileged Place of the Poor

If in the Lukan community the poor were the disenfranchised and the repressed from a socioeconomic viewpoint, their status is radically different from God's perspective. In the divine economy of salvation they are no longer reduced to insignificance; rather they are the special recipients of God's favor. They are raised up to a privileged place in God's eyes, and hence in the community of believers.

The privileged place of the poor is dominant in the first several chapters of Luke's Gospel. It is celebrated from the very beginning in the infancy narrative as the drama of salvation dawns (chs. 1–2). "Little people" play a central role in the births of John the Baptist and of Jesus, both of which take place in the most unlikely of circumstances. What God has already accomplished in them and all the humble is proclaimed in Mary's canticle (1:46-55). Their fortunes are reversed, as are those of the proud and rich. This same theme is then echoed in the preaching of the Baptist, who adds specific ethical instructions (3:4-6, 10-14). In his inaugural discourse Jesus announces that God's spirit has anointed him to proclaim good news to the poor (4:16-20). This mission is then fulfilled in word and deed. In the Sermon on the Plain Jesus tells the poor that they are the blessed ones in God's kingdom (6:20-36). Then to John's disciples Jesus recounts what he has already done: The blind see, the lame walk, and the poor have the good news preached to them (7:18-23). Each of these passages from the early chapters of Luke's Gospel will be discussed as well as a text that comes toward the end of the narrative and is about another "little person," the poor widow who has contributed "all the living that she had" to the temple treasury (21:1-4).

A. The *"Little People"* in the Infancy Narrative (chs. 1–2)

Following the prologue addressed to Theophilus, a person of some means, the cast of characters, Zechariah and Elizabeth, Joseph and Mary, Simeon and Anna, comes mainly from the lower class. They are all faithful Jews in Palestine before the birth of Jesus. Each of these experiences in his or her own way the power of God. Zechariah, from "the priestly division of Abijah" (1:5) was one of the ordinary priests who lived and worked among the peasants in the villages. As such his status was inferior to that of the ruling high priests. Both Zechariah and Elizabeth live with the distressing circumstance that they have no offspring and are not likely to have any in the future, since Elizabeth is barren and both of them are advanced in years. But the Lord brings joy and gladness to their lives by giving them a child, who is named John. This same Lord promises Mary a son, but this seems impossible to her since she has no husband. But the Lord provides in the way announced by the angel: "The Holy Spirit will come upon you" (1:35). Joseph plays his part as Mary's betrothed by being with her in Bethlehem, where the child is born. Simeon, a righteous and devout man, awaits the restoration of Israel, which is to come with the Messiah. His hope is fulfilled when he holds in his arms the child Jesus. Anna, an eighty-four-year-old widow, also sees Jesus and speaks about him to all who are looking for the redemption of Jerusalem.

In contrast to this central cast taken from the "little people," there are the politically powerful, for example, Herod, king of Judea (1:5); Caesar Augustus, the Roman emperor (2:1); and Quirinius, the governor of Syria (2:2). From the imperial rule of Caesar to the local hegemony of Herod, the political potentates represent the old political order that brought oppression and violence, repeated conquest and burdensome tribute, to the Palestinian Jews. In contrast, the birth of Jesus inaugurated a whole new order supplanting the oppressive authority of the "kings of the Gentiles" (22:25) with self-giving service.[1]

Jesus is the hero, the main character in Luke's Gospel narrative. His birth is portrayed without pretension; humble circumstances rather than regal splendor surround this event. When he is born Jesus is placed in a manger (2:7, 16), since there is no place for him in the inn (2:7). The lack of accommodations for his birth foreshadows the homelessness of Jesus mentioned later in the Gospel, for he is a wandering preacher continually on the journey with no home for himself. He tells those who desire to follow him that the Son of Man has no place to lay his head (9:59).

Those who come to visit the infant Jesus in the manger are not the socially respectable Wise Men, as in Matthew's Gospel, but poor shepherds from the field (2:8, 15, 18). Later, when Jesus is taken to the Temple, his parents offer in sacrifice "a pair of turtledoves, or two young pigeons" (2:24). The implication here is that Mary and Joseph could not afford the one-year-old lamb, a more costly offering. Jesus, his parents, and the shepherds who first visit him are all of humble origin. What Luke communicates to his readers through the presentation of these "little people" at the beginning of his story is that those without power, wealth, or influence are the ones who enjoy God's special favor. Celebrating this divine predilection with particular solemnity is Mary's prayer, the *Magnificat*.

B. The Magnificat: *Eschatological Reversal* (1:46-55)

That God acts decisively on behalf of the lowly is proclaimed by Mary in the *Magnificat*. In this hymn of praise "God's fulfillment of all that he has planned for creation and humankind is seen as beginning with Jesus' conception."[2] Taken over from the tradition, this is the first Lukan statement about how God's favor rests upon the poor and is turned against the rich who reject God and oppress others.

Mary's canticle (1:46-55) is a response to Elizabeth's canticle (1:42-45) following upon the two annunciations, that of John the

[1]For a recent sociohistorical study of the infancy narratives, see Richard A. Horsley, *The Liberation of Christmas: The Infancy Narratives in Social Context* (New York: Crossroad, 1989).

[2]Robert J. Karris, *Luke: Artist and Theologian* (New York: Paulist, 1985) 52.

Baptist (1:5-25) and that of Jesus (1:26-38). When Mary, pregnant with the child to be called the Son of God, encounters Elizabeth, who is in the sixth month with her child, John, Elizabeth raises her voice in praise of Mary because she is the mother of the Lord. Then Mary transfers the praise to God, the one who has the principal role in the drama of salvation, by recalling God's mighty deeds.

The *Magnificat,* like the other hymns in Luke 1-2, probably came from the Greek-speaking Jewish Christian community influenced by Jerusalem Christianity.[3] It is included by Luke to proclaim how God has acted in the life of one lowly yet significant person, Mary (1:46-50). What Mary has experienced symbolizes how God acts globally toward all people (vv. 51-53), specifically toward Israel, God's faithful people (vv. 54-55).

God has looked upon Mary, God's servant, in her "low estate" (*tapeinōsis,* v. 48). Used in the Hebrew Scriptures to refer to a woman's barrenness, the term "lowliness/humiliation" describes Mary's situation as a young virgin, a female dependent in a patriarchal society. She is a handmaid, literally, a female slave, of the Lord (vv. 38, 48) and a virgin (v. 27). For Luke the virginity of Mary "was like the barrenness of the OT women: both constituted a human impossibility which only the might of God could overcome."[4] God, the Mighty One (*ho dunatos,* v. 49; cf. v. 35), responds to Mary's lowliness by doing "great things" (*megala*) for her (v. 49). Through God's power Mary conceives a child, who is to be called Christ the Lord. In this way Mary is the recipient of God's mercy (v. 50); God is indeed Mary's Savior (v. 47). What Mary experiences is a reversal of her condition. Considered lowly by societal standards, she is the recipient of the great things of God. What this woman has experienced becomes a powerful symbol of how God acts on behalf of all others "who fear him" (v. 50). As God has done for Mary, so also God reverses the fortunes of all those who turn to divine mercy.

The next verses proclaim that God acts for all those who depend on God and against those who refuse to do so (vv. 51-53). Speaking about God from a human point of view, the author says

---

[3] See Raymond E. Brown, *The Birth of the Messiah: A Commentary on the Infancy Narratives in Matthew and Luke* (New York: Doubleday, 1977) 355.

[4] Brown, *Messiah,* 361.

that God "has shown might with his arm" (v. 51). The Greek verb translated in this phrase as "has shown" (*epoiēsen*) was used a few lines earlier to indicate what God "did" for Mary (v. 49). The anthropomorphism of God's arm symbolizes the "strength or power (see Exod 6:6; Deut 4:34; Isa 40:10; 51:5, 9; 53:1), by which he reverses the condition in which human beings find themselves or which they have fashioned for themselves."[5]

Five reversals are effected: The proud are scattered "in the imagination of their hearts" (v. 51b); the mighty are put down from their thrones (v. 52a); the lowly are raised to high places (v. 52b); the hungry are filled with good things (v. 53a); and the rich are sent away empty (v. 53b). God acts against the proud, the mighty, and the rich; God acts in favor of the lowly and the hungry. In their arrogant self-sufficiency the proud trust in themselves (cf. 18:9-14); they look down on others but not up to God. In their claim to authority the mighty are like earthly kings who lord it over their people (22:25). They fail to acknowledge God who is the "Mighty One." By contrast the "lowly" (*tapeinoi,* the same term used to describe Mary) are the "poor ones" who fear God, depend upon God, and have their eyes cast on God. The reversal of the first three groups announced here prepares the reader for the judgment pronounced later in the parable of the guests at the wedding feast (14:7-11) and the parable of the Pharisee and tax collector (18:9-14). Both of these parables conclude with the saying: "For everyone who exalts himself will be humbled, but the one who humbles himself will be exalted."

In the last two reversals the hungry and rich are addressed. The "emptiness" of the rich is suggested by the literary parallelism with the hungry who are "filled" (cf. the servants who are sent away "empty" when they try to collect the owner's share of the crop from the wicked tenants, 20:10-11). The plight of the hungry is repeatedly dramatized later in the person of Lazarus, who longs for table scraps (16:19-31); in the weary crowds who follow Jesus to "a lonely place" (9:12); in those who are concerned about what to eat (12:22); and in the beggars, the crippled, the lame, and the blind, whose nourishment depends upon receiving a dinner invitation (14:12-24). The blessedness of the hungry is

[5]Fitzmyer, *Luke*, I, 368.

proclaimed in the second Lukan beatitude (6:20). The life of the rich is opposite that of the hungry in almost every way. For the rich are those whose wealth chokes the word they have received (8:14). They are those who identify their life's security with the quality of their possessions (12:16-21) and who fail to be generous in the face of the poor (16:19-31). Judgment is pronounced on the rich in the first Lukan woe (6:24). It is interesting to note that the same term for the "good things" (*agatha*) of the wealthy man in the parable of the rich fool is used for the promise made to the hungry in the *Magnificat*. Whereas the rich fool accumulates "good things" for his own security, God gives "good things" to the hungry. From a broader societal perspective, the goods of this earth are controlled by relatively few people, who maintain their privilege by perpetuating structures of injustice and exclusion. God, however, intervenes on the side of the many oppressed and becomes their advocate.

The Greek verbs used in Mary's canticle for the exercise of God's judgment and saving activity are in the aorist tense and are translated in past time. These aorist verbs can be taken as references to genuine past events. On the lips of Mary the reference is to how God has acted generally with Israel, the *anawim,* and specifically with her who has been chosen to bear the Savior. From the perspective of the evangelist, we have in the *Magnificat* a retrospective view of how God has already brought salvation to others through the life and career of Jesus, although the reader is yet to hear about these saving events in the narrative to follow. Above all, many of these verbs, for example, "to exalt" (*hypsoō*) those of low degree, apply to the action of God, who has reversed Jesus' own fortune by raising him from death to life. God "exalts (*hypsōsen*) him at his right hand as Leader and Savior" (Acts 5:31).

Later in the infancy narrative Simeon makes clear to Mary that her child "is set for the fall and rising of many in Israel, and for a sign that is spoken against" (2:34). As such, Jesus is "the stone which the builders rejected" who "has become the keystone of the structure" (20:17). Those subject to downfall are the proud, the mighty, and the rich; those uplifted are the lowly and the hungry. This privileged place of the poor is brought about in the ministry of Jesus, whose appearance in public life is prepared by the preaching of John the Baptist.

C. The Preaching of the Baptist (3:4-14)

The word of God comes to John the Baptist while he is in the wilderness (3:2). The Baptist does not have a high socioeconomic status as is suggested by Jesus later in the narrative. John is neither "gorgeously appareled" nor does he "live in luxury" as do those in kings' courts (7:25). John is called to proclaim " a baptism of repentance for the forgiveness of sins" (3:3). The function of his mission is disclosed further through poetic language from the prophet Isaiah, which is reminiscent of the reversal of fortunes in the *Magnificat*. The valleys are to be filled, the mountains leveled, and the winding paths made straight (3:5). Although the poetic imagery should not be pressed too far, the expression "every mountain and hill shall be brought low [*tapeinōthēsetai*]" does suggest the humbling of the proud (cf. 1:52; 14:11; 18:14).[6] In this way their road is made straight so that they, too, "shall see the salvation of God" (3:6).

In his call for repentance the Baptist requires some evidence to show that conversion is genuine. He tells the crowds who come out to be baptized that it is not sufficient to rely upon claims of ethnic identity such as "we have Abraham as our father" (3:8). John also warns against a feigned repentance by calling those who are fleeing "the wrath to come" (3:7) to produce fruits worthy of repentance. By using the image of an ax being laid to the root of the tree, he announces that an eschatological judgment already being made in the present will sort out and destroy those not bearing fruit (3:9). This proclamation sets the stage for the crucial question, raised successively by the crowds, the tax collectors, and the soldiers: "What are we to do?" (3:10, 12, 14).[7] This is a question of salvation, of life and death, raised later by the rich man who wants to share in everlasting life (18:18) and by the Pentecost crowd in Jerusalem at the end of Peter's first sermon in Acts. Peter's response, "you must reform and be baptized . . . that your sins may be forgiven" (Acts 2:38), echoes the preaching of John (Luke 3:3).

---

[6] See I. Howard Marshall, *The Gospel of Luke,* The New International Greek Testament Commentary (Exeter: Paternoster, 1978) 137.

[7] A variant reading for 3:10 has a fuller question: "What are we to do in order that we may be saved?" (cf. Acts 16:30).

To the crowd's query, John replies: Share your coat and your food with those who are without. The term used for coat is that of an undergarment. Normally a peasant or poor person would have two such tunics, one for the Sabbath and one for daily use. Yet even a person with so little is called to share. Those having meager possessions are called to share with those who are in greater need. Because of their own experience of want, the poor sharing with the poor creates a special kind of solidarity.[8] Later in Acts the disciples at Antioch follow the principle of sharing "each according to ability" as they give for the famine relief (Acts 11:29). If even the less well off are to share with others, how much more so is the obligation of giving incumbent upon the wealthy. Later in the Gospel a rich man lavishly dressed and sumptuously fed refuses to do just this. After the divine judgment sends him to a place of torment, his threefold appeal to Father Abraham (16:24, 27, 30) is of no avail (see 3:8). Fruits of repentance are not forthcoming in his life; hence his plaintive cries in death are not heard, while Zacchaeus' generous sharing with the poor enables him to become a true "son of Abraham" (19:9). For the Baptist, preparing for the time of salvation requires sharing with the needy encountered during the concrete circumstances of one's earthly life.

After the crowds, two specific groups, the toll collectors and the soldiers, ask what their response should be. The toll collectors, as distinguished from those who solicited direct taxes such as the poll tax and land tax, were those engaged in the collection of indirect taxes such as tolls, tariffs, imposts, and customs.[9] They are not told to leave their profession. Instead, their repentance requires them to resist the natural temptation of their vocation: Take nothing beyond what is authorized (3:13). John implies that dishonesty is common among them and that this has to cease. Then come the soldiers. During the Baptist's generation these would be Jewish men enlisted in the service of Herod Antipas,

---

[8] See Wolfgang Stegemann, *The Gospel and the Poor* (Philadelphia: Fortress, 1984; trans. Matthew J. O'Connell from *Das Evangelium und die Armen: Uber den Ursprung der Theologie der Armen in Neuen Testament* [München: Kaiser, 1981]) 27. Stegemann comments that the experience of the poor "included a solidarity which meant sharing the last morsel in the face of common want (Luke 3:11)."

[9] Fitzmyer, *Luke,* I, 469.

one of the sons of Herod the Great. The soldiers are given a three-fold injunction: Do not extort, do not accuse falsely for gain, and be satisfied with your pay. John warns them against economic misdeeds toward others and discontent regarding their wages. Extortion was evidently a problem at the time, as this term comes up also with Zacchaeus, who may have been guilty of this injustice. To those treated dishonestly in this way, Zacchaeus promises to repay fourfold (19:8).

John's ethical instructions, while not disturbing the existing social order—no one is asked to leave his profession or to give away all his possessions—do advocate a genuine concern for one's neighbor. The specific actions that the Baptist prescribes for his fellow Jews were also appropriate for the Christian readers of the Gospel. The community was expected to bear good fruit. To each member the question "What are we to do?" was addressed. The connection made in this passage between the kerygma and ethical conduct says much about how the call to repentance was to be lived out in everyday life, particularly as this related to the right use and dangers of possessions. As the Gospel unfolds, the preaching of John to the crowds is taken up and presented by Luke, often in a more radical form through various commandments of Jesus (see 6:30, 34, 35; 12:33; 14:12-14; 16:9; 18:22).

D. Jesus' Preaching of Good News to the Poor at Nazareth (4:16-20)

John the Baptist preaches good news to the people (3:18), preparing them for the coming of one who, he says, is "mightier than I" (3:16). Then, after the imprisonment of the Baptist (3:20), Jesus, the coming one in whom the new age is realized, appears on the scene and is baptized by John. During his baptism Jesus receives the Holy Spirit, an event interpreted by a heavenly voice that underscores the unique relationship between God and Jesus. Jesus is God's beloved Son (3:22). Having received the Spirit, Jesus is empowered to carry out his divine mission. In this baptismal scene the voice is addressed to Jesus alone, but later in the Nazareth episode the nature of Jesus' mission will be announced publicly.

After the baptism the narrator traces the genealogy of God's Son back to Adam (3:23-38), and gives Jesus' own struggle with a false understanding of what it means to be God's Son (4:1-13). In the temptation scene Jesus is faced with using his privileged relationship with God as Son to serve his own needs by using his power to change stones into bread in order to satisfy his hunger, by accepting power over all the world's kingdoms at the cost of worshiping Satan, and by displaying the awesomeness of his power through a daring jump from the Temple parapet and a dramatic rescue. Jesus' mission is neither self-serving nor is it under the manipulation of Satanic power. His mission is from God and is motivated by the Spirit to preach good news to the poor.

After the temptation scene Jesus returns "in the power of the Spirit into Galilee" (4:14) and makes it a practice to teach (see the imperfect *edidasken* in v. 15) in the synagogues, particularly one at Nazareth, on the Sabbath. For Luke, one of these visits stands out among the others and functions as a programmatic statement for the rest of the Gospel narrative. Citing from Isaiah, Jesus announces that the Spirit of the Lord has anointed him "to preach good news to the poor" (4:18). Luke unfolds this momentous public presentation of Jesus for his readers by giving the central content of Jesus' proclamation (4:16-21) and by telling how his preaching is received, first by marvelous praise (4:22; cf. v. 15), then by obstinate rejection (4:23-30). In the citation from Isaiah four elements central to the narrative stand out: It is a statement from Scripture by the highest human authority containing his commission and offering a preview to the rest of the story. Robert Tannehill comments: "As Scripture, it is viewed as testimony to God's purpose. As a statement by Jesus, it comes from the human character of highest authority within the narrative. It is a statement of what the Lord has sent Jesus to do, i.e., a statement of Jesus' commission, which should lead us to expect that it is also a preview of what Jesus will in fact be doing in the following narrative."[10]

The Scripture cited is a conflation of two Isaian texts (61:1; 58:6) joined by the Greek word *aphesis* (4:18c, 18d), a term translated here by "release" (v. 18c) and "liberty" (v. 18d) and fre-

---

[10]Tannehill, *Unity*, 61.

quently used elsewhere in Luke's Gospel and Acts, where it is translated as "forgiveness" (1:77; 3:3; 24:47; Acts 2:38; 5:31; 10:43; 13:38; 26:18). First, Jesus presents himself as consciously aware of the influence of the Spirit upon him who has anointed him (cf. Acts 10:38). The anointing is more prophetic (see 4:25-27) than messianic, although the two are not mutually exclusive. Then Jesus gives the purpose of his mission, namely, "to preach good news,"[11] an expression explained in concrete fashion by the next two infinitival constructions: "to proclaim release [*aphesis*] to the captives and recovery of sight to the blind" and "to set at liberty [*aphesis*] those who are oppressed" (4:18). The final infinitival phrase, "to proclaim the acceptable year of the Lord," also depending grammatically on the verb "he sent," summarizes in Jubilee language (explained below) the purpose of Jesus' commission.

Each of these expressions merits a closer look. The verb "to preach good news" (*euangelizō*), used several times in Luke-Acts, occurs again at the end of the Nazareth story. Jesus tells the crowds, "I must preach the good news of the kingdom of God to the other cities also" (4:43). The kingdom of God, not further explained in this, the first Lukan occurrence, is the kerygma, that is, the preaching of Jesus. Hence Jesus is the herald of God's kingdom. The good news heard by the poor (*ptōchoi*) is itself the kingdom of God. Who are the poor addressed here? Many attempts have been made to identify the poor as one particular social, economic, or religious group or as all Israel.[12] Within Luke's narrative those who are poor have many faces and experience poverty in different ways.

The poor are first and foremost those who lack adequate material things to meet their basic needs for food, shelter, and clothing (see 6:20; 7:22; 14:13, 21; 16:20, 22; 18:22; 19:8; 21:3). These poor live in poverty through no choice of their own. The good news to the poor also applies to those who voluntarily choose to give up their possessions, home, and livelihood in order to fol-

---

[11]Following the LXX, "To announce good news" goes with "he sent me" rather than with "he anointed me."

[12]See David Peter Seccombe (*Possessions and the Poor in Luke-Acts,* Studien zum Neuen Testament und seiner Umwelt. Series B, vol. 6 [Linz: 1982] 24–43). Seccombe discusses each of these interpretations and then opts for an identification with Israel as a whole.

low Jesus (5:11; 18:28) or who respond to Jesus' command to "sell what you have and give alms" (12:33). The poor are the economically oppressed both within Israel and without. During his public ministry Jesus begins by proclaiming salvation within Israel. This is God's mission for Jesus, as Peter tells Cornelius: "You know the word which [God] sent to Israel, preaching the good news of peace by Jesus Christ (he is Lord of all)" (Acts 10:36). The verb *euangelizō* used here and in Luke 4:18 provides yet another link between the two passages (see above). However, the poor are not limited to Israel. Just as the prophets Elijah and Elisha were sent to Gentiles in distress (4:25-27), so also Jesus proclaims the good news to the poor among the Gentiles, to those beyond his own geographical, cultural, and racial boundaries (see 4:43).

Who are the poor? Continuing with the divinely authoritative word of Isaiah, Jesus names the poor as the captives, the blind, and the bound. Literally the captives are prisoners of war; metaphorically, they are those enslaved because of debts. But as their debts mount the debtors would eventually lose their property and, thus unable to pay, would themselves be imprisoned. The captives are promised their freedom, their release (*aphesis*). Occurring twice in this passage, *aphesis* is the same term used frequently in the narrative for "release of sins." Forgiveness from God to those enslaved by their sinfulness was the most profound kind of release the readers of the Gospel experienced.

The blind receive their sight. This foreshadows, in part, Jesus' healing ministry to those who are physically blind. On a broader level, light serves as a symbol for the dawn of salvation, inaugurated with Jesus' mission. The rich symbolic use of light in Isaiah (Isa 42:6-7; 49:6; 58:8, 10) plays an important role in Luke-Acts (Luke 2:32; 3:6; 4:18; Acts 13:47; 26:17-18). Simeon pronounces that the child Jesus is "a revealing light to the Gentiles" (2:32). In him all people "shall see the salvation of God" (3:6), as the Baptist later proclaims. Thus Jesus realizes and fulfills what is said about light, healing, and release in Isaiah 42:6-7: "I have given you as . . . a light to the nations, to open the eyes that are blind, to bring out the prisoners from the dungeon, from the prison those who sit in darkness" (cf. Isa 49:6; 58:8, 10). Here opening the eyes of the blind is related to becoming a "light to the nations." In Acts, Paul and Barnabas also explain their own commission from the Lord, using light as an image for salvation: "I have set you to be a light for the Gentiles, that you may bring salvation to the uttermost parts of the earth" (Acts 13:47; see Isa 49:6). Before King Agrippa, Paul summarizes his mission, using themes similar to those found in Jesus' inaugural sermon: He reports that the Lord sent him "to open [the Gentiles'] eyes, that they may turn from darkness to light and from the power of Satan to God, that they may receive forgiveness of sins [*aphesin hamartiōn*]" (Acts 26:18). The Lord tells Paul that bringing light means freedom from the bondage of Satan and forgiveness of sins, two hallmarks of Jesus' ministry. As the bearer of light, Jesus brings physical sight and salvation and in this way serves as a model for others called to be heralds of the gospel.

The downtrodden are sent away "in liberty" (*en aphesei*). The downtrodden are those oppressed by physical and mental disorders understood to be caused by Satan. The Nazareth pericope is framed by two encounters of conflict between Jesus and Satan. In the temptation scene Jesus refuses to submit to demonic enticements (4:1-13); in a Capernaum synagogue he drives out a demonic spirit oppressing a downtrodden man (4:33-37). Later in the narrative Jesus brings release to a daughter of Abraham "whom Satan bound" (13:10-17). Luke has Peter summarize Jesus' activity as "healing all that were oppressed [*katadunasteuomenous*] by the devil" (Acts 10:38). Hence, Jesus' healings and exorcisms are significant dimensions of his mission in bringing "release."

The vivid imagery helps us to fill out more completely our picture of the poor. They are those in prison because of their indebtedness, in darkness without salvation; they are those afflicted by sickness and held in bondage by Satan. The good news for these poor means release from their oppression, a release realized in Jesus.

Concluding his reading from Isaiah, Jesus explains his mission as being sent "to proclaim the Lord's favorable year." Although this language is reminiscent of the biblical Jubilee year (Lev 25:10; 2 Kgs 6:2), a time when lost ancestral property was returned and debts were released, the narrator does not specifically call attention to Jesus' pronouncement as taking place during a Jubilee year, nor does Jesus demand the return of family property.[13] Jesus' Sabbath appearance in the synagogue is not unusual, for he is there according to "his custom" (4:16).

The Lord's acceptable year refers not so much to a specific Jubilee year but to the present time, that is, the time of salvation (12:56; 19:44). This is the time when the reign of God is being announced (4:43), a reign in which Jesus has been entrusted with royal authority by his Father (22:29-30). The public life and ministry of Jesus is the time of God's Jubilee. In the words of one author, "Jesus has come to announce the great Jubilee of God's final deliverance of his people."[14]

After Jesus has finished reading from the scroll, those present in the synagogue have their eyes "fixed on him (4:20), yet as the narrative unfolds their initial admiration (4:21) turns to indignation (4:28), blinding them to the salvation now being fulfilled (4:21), even, or especially, among those outside of Israel (4:25-27). Jesus' announcement of his mission is indeed being fulfilled "today" (4:21), so Luke's readers could expect that the divine plan announced in Isaiah would be realized from now on in the narrative life of Jesus. The hostile rejection Jesus experiences from his hometown folks imprisoned by their own ethnocentricity foreshadows the rejection Jesus will experience from his home nation. With the repetition of one key word, the narrator contrasts on the one hand the divine initiative of proclaiming an "acceptable [*dekton*] year of the Lord" with the human rejection of this initiative, "no prophet is acceptable [*dektos*] in his own country" (4:24; cf. Matt 13:57; Mark 6:4, who have *atimos*) on the other hand. Jesus the prophet proclaims a year acceptable to the Lord, but he himself is not acceptable to his people.[15] The far-reaching implications of Jesus' proclamation of good news to the poor threatens those who would claim superiority over others and find security for themselves because of their self-conceived privileged positions of ethnic identity. After Jesus' inaugural discourse at Nazareth the narrator relates a number of healing miracles, call

[13]For further discussion see Sharon H. Ringe, *Jesus, Liberation, and the Biblical Jubilee*, Overtures to Biblical Theology 19 (Philadelphia: Fortress, 1985).

[14]Seccombe, *Possessions*, 56.

[15]Johnson, *Function*, 94.

stories, and disputes with the Pharisees. This leads us to the great discourse, the Sermon on the Plain, during the course of which Jesus calls the poor "blessed."

E. The Sermon on the Plain (6:20-36)

We are including the discussion of the Beatitudes and woes from Luke's Sermon on the Plain in this chapter because the focus is indeed on the privileged place of the poor. This passage could also be included in the next chapter, on discipleship and possessions, since the Beatitudes are addressed specifically to the disciples. However, as we will mention below, the crowds are also present, hearing what Jesus has to say. Finally, the reversal of fortunes proclaimed in Mary's jubilant hymn, the first text considered in this chapter, is taken up in the Sermon on the Plain and recast in language of blessedness for the poor and woe for the rich. The vocabulary of being hungry, being filled, and being rich (*peinōntas, eneplēsen, ploutountas*) in 1:53 is taken up and reformulated in both the Beatitudes in 6:21 (*peinōntes*) and the woes in 6:24, 25 (*plousiois, hoi empeplēsmenoi, peinasete*).

Luke sets the scene for Jesus' great sermon on a level plain down from the mountain (6:17), where Jesus has just spent the night in prayer. The next day he selects twelve from among the disciples to be his apostles (6:12-16). The first part of Jesus' Sermon on the Plain is in the form of four beatitudes and four woes (6:20-26), followed by a radical call to love one's enemies (6:27-35), teachings about not judging another person (6:36-42), sayings about the link between one's deeds and one's heart (6:43-45), and a parable about putting words into practice (6:46-49).

1. *The Audience.* For whom is Jesus' instruction intended? The narrator clearly directs our attention to the disciples. In verse 20 Jesus begins to speak with the dramatic gesture of "raising his eyes to his disciples." Apparently, then, the disciples are the immediate focus of this address. However, they are not the only ones present. There is also a large multitude of people who have come for the explicit purpose of hearing Jesus (6:17-18) and trying to touch him, "for power came forth from him" (6:19). We are given a picture of large numbers from all over gathered around him along with " a great crowd of his disciples" (6:17; cf. 6:20). Fur-

ther references to the crowd come just after the fourth woe, in verse 27, "But I say to you that hear . . ." and in 7:1, "After he had ended all his sayings in the hearing of the people. . . ." So crowds are present; they have come to hear, and Jesus responds by teaching. Hence we should not make too sharp a separation between the disciples and the others. The Beatitudes do apply in a special way to the disciples, for they are economically poor, having left everything to follow Jesus (5:11, 28). These same Beatitudes also apply to all those from the crowd who voluntarily leave their possessions as they answer the call to become disciples. They are included among those called blessed.

For whose ears are the woes intended? Who are the rich, the well fed, those laughing? There is no clue up to this point in the narrative that any of Jesus' disciples, having left all, return to a life of possessions or become rich. The rich are others in the crowd to whom the invitation and challenge to discipleship goes out. In Luke's time the rich could be either those who were interested in joining the community but were hesitant because of their wealth, or they could be those already in the community, whether as leaders or members, who took comfort in their riches at the expense of the needy.[16]

One further comment should be made about the crowds present. They come from a wide geographical area, from "all Judea and Jerusalem" (6:17), representative of the people Israel. They are also from "the coast of Tyre and Sidon," Gentile territory, representative of the universal scope of Jesus' message from the narrator's perspective.

2. *The Beatitudes* (6:20-23). The first three Lukan beatitudes consist of two parts: The first names an existing situation of human misery, the second promises future reversal and compensation. The human misery identified by these three beatitudes refers to one group: The poor are the hungry and those who mourn. The Greek term for poor, *ptōchoi,* means, according to

---

[16]It is incorrect to interpret the Lukan Jesus' warnings about the rich and the dangers of wealth as directed specifically and exclusively against the Church leaders of Luke's time. Such an interpretation has been advocated by Hans Joachim Degenhardt, *Lukas, Evangelist der Armen: Besitz und Besitzverzicht in den lukanischen Schriften* (Stuttgart: Katholisches Bibelwerk, 1965), 215-216. Also, see below, chapter 3, pp. 71-72.

many commentators, those who are completely destitute,[17] that is, so poor as to have to beg (contrast the other Greek term for poor, *penēs,* which means one who works), those who are economically deprived.[18]

In stark contrast to the painful reality of their present condition, the poor are called "blessed" (*makarioi*). The good fortune, the happiness, even the "good luck" of the poor is acclaimed. Why? The reasons not given for their blessedness are as enlightening as those that are. The poor are called blessed (1) not because of the miserable condition in which they find themselves—poverty in itself is not acclaimed as a state of happiness, (2) not because of any repentance, virtue, or internal disposition they might have—no prior repentance or virtue is required, and (3) not because they are doers of the Law or faithful to the covenant— their status as keepers of the Law is not addressed. Without any prior qualifications the poor are called happy for one reason: They are the recipients of the reign of God. To them God's message of salvation, realized in the kingdom preaching of Jesus, is made available. Already now the poor, particularly the disciples whose way of life is decidedly marked by following Jesus, experience salvation. There is also a future dimension to their blessed condition. In the eschatological future, the poor will enjoy the fullness of God's reign. This promise of salvation is made to them unconditionally. The first three beatitudes present God's attitude toward the poor, not that of the world. As Jan Lambrecht comments: "What is primary in these beatitudes is God's free gift, his grace, which is always present even before any human action. Jesus proclaims and reveals this breakthrough of divine mercy, God's new initiative."[19]

Jesus' address to the poor is intensified by the use of the second-person plural: ". . . is yours, . . . you shall be . . ., you shall . . .," unlike Matthew, who has the third-person plural. The encounter between Jesus and the disciples as well as the crowd who come to hear is direct, personal, and given with the assurance

[17]See the differing perspective of Malina, discussed above, pp. 29-31, according to whom there were no destitute people in the first century c.e.

[18]See above, pp. 46-47.

[19]Jan Lambrecht, *The Sermon on the Mount: Proclamation and Exhortation,* Good News Studies 14 (Wilmington: Michael Glazier, 1985) 56.

of his unique authority as God's anointed one. By preaching to the poor this message of salvation, Jesus realizes the heart of his mission, given in the programmatic statement of 4:18. In the hearing of their blessedness as participants in God's reign, the poor are being given the good news.

In the second and third beatitudes Luke accentuates the present experience of those who hunger and mourn by the significant adverb "now." The present life, the "now," is set in opposition to what will unfold in the future, after death.[20] You who experience physical hunger now will be satisfied; you who mourn now will laugh. A mourner "is one afflicted with evil who by mourning protests the presence of evil."[21] The content of the future promise is very concrete; it corresponds to the longed-for reversal of physical hunger and emotional distress. Later in the narrative, at the festive meal of loaves and fishes, Jesus alleviates the crowd's hunger: "They ate and all were filled" (9:17). This concrete action is a direct response to present need and a symbolic representation of the eschatological fulfillment promised in the second beatitude. The feeding becomes a preliminary participation in the messianic meal.

The fourth beatitude focuses on the abusive rejection suffered by followers of Jesus at the hands of others. As such, it identifies the listeners as disciples of Jesus. Thus, this beatitude adds a new dimension to the understanding of the poor. To be poor is to be a disciple who experiences rejection by others because of his or her close allegiance to the Son of Man. As the prophets were rejected (6:23), as Jesus the prophet was rejected (4:28-30), so do the disciples experience rejection.[22] In this is their poverty; in this is their blessedness. Faced with a fourfold affront—being hated, ostracized, insulted—all this for the sake of the Son of Man—and having their name rejected as evil, these disciples are blessed because they will have a great reward in heaven. Confronted with much adversity, the disciples are motivated by their present commitment and relationship to Jesus; their future reward is in heaven.

---

[20]See Lambrecht, *Sermon*, 71.

[21]Bruce J. Malina, *The New Testament World: Insights from Cultural Anthropology* (Atlanta: John Knox) 85.

[22]See Johnson, *Function*, 134–135.

God's attitude toward the poor is clear. They do have a privileged place. Singled out from among all others, they are the ones called blessed. Fully aware of their present condition of distress, Jesus offers them the fullness of God's kingdom, where they will be satisfied, where they will laugh, and where they will leap for joy.

3. *The Woes* (6:24-26). The other group of people addressed in the opening part of the Sermon on the Plain enjoy a present lifestyle free from want, hunger, or sorrow. They are the rich, the well fed, those who laugh, and those spoken well of. Addressed with the ominous interjection, "Woe to you," these privileged ones in society stand under divine judgment. Those addressed as rich (cf. 1:53) are not accused of any extraordinary injustice or callousness. It is simply a matter of fact that they have had it good in this life. They have already received in this life all the consolation they are going to get; they have received what their money and possessions have provided. In Luke's Gospel the rich are easily recognized by their luxurious dress (7:25; 16:19), by their sumptuous banquets (12:19; 16:19), and in general by their extravagant living (7:25). The behavior of the rich is characteristically selfish (12:19; 16:19-31). Not only are they persons of wealth, they are members of the elite, well placed as patrons. Luke gives only one instance of a rich person who shows generosity and that is Zacchaeus, the chief tax collector of Jericho (19:1-10). In the *Magnificat,* the misfortune of the rich from God's perspective has already been pronounced: They will be "sent away empty" without the material comforts of this life, but much worse, without God's promise of blessedness. The address of the "woes" in the second-person plural again brings into focus the listening crowd, especially those who are well off. Luke's concern here may well be with "the rich members of his community whom persecution unmasks as too attached to their possessions."[23]

The last three woes identify other life experiences that characterize the rich: They have adequate resources to be well fed, even to "feast sumptuously" (16:19); they can afford to "laugh," even to be boastful in their own contented feeling of self-satisfaction

[23]Robert J. Karris, "Rich and Poor: The Lukan *Sitz-im-Leben,*" in Charles H. Talbert (ed.), *Perspectives on Luke-Acts,* Perspectives in Religious Studies (Edinburgh: T & T Clark, 1978) 112-125, 118.

while being indifferent to others. Finally, the rich receive the adulation of others who are impressed by wealth. None of the rich portrayed here are called blessed, nor is anything said to them about theirs being the kingdom of God (6:20).

4. *Love Your Enemies, Giving, and Lending* (6:27-36). The second part of Jesus' sermon, introduced with "But I say to you," an expression underscoring his unique authority, begins with the imperative "Love your enemies" (6:27; see v. 35). The next three imperatives specify the kind of enemies the disciples can expect to encounter: those who hate you, who curse you, and who maltreat you. To love one's enemies means to "do good to those who hate you, bless those who curse you, pray for those who abuse you" (6:27-28). Who is my enemy? Everyone who acts with hostility toward me. Looking back to the woes, one's enemy may be the rich, the well fed, and those who laugh. With the fourfold imperatives for discipleship in 6:27-28, coming after the fourfold beatitudes in 6:20-23 and the fourfold woes in 6:24-26, the reader appreciates the symmetrical artistry of the narrator.

In the next series of teachings still under the heading of "love your enemies," there are instructions specifically relating to sharing material things, giving alms, not seeking restitution, and lending money. Thus, the focus of discussion in Luke's sermon shifts from the poor and the rich viewed from the perspective of their status before God to the use of one's possessions viewed from the perspective of one's obligations as a disciple to others.

In tandem with Jesus' teaching about nonretaliation when one's person is violated by a hostile blow (6:29a), there is the instruction not to prevent another from taking one's own undergarment (chit*ō*n), after one's outer garment (*himation*) has already been taken (6:29b). No motivation, whether justifiable or not, is given for the garment-seizing action of the aggressor. It could be "the act of a thief, or of a person in need, or of one seizing a garment in pledge because of a legality (see Exod 22:25-26; Deut 24:10-17; Amos 2:8)."[24] Given the thematic note sounded at the outset about loving one's enemies, the reader can understand this to be a hostile, probably unjustified action. Whatever the case, the offending party's motivation is irrelevant. There can only be one response

[24]Fitzmyer, *Luke*, I, 639.

for the disciple, namely, to be willing to part with the inner garment as well. The sense of this verse is not so much about a conscious decision to share one's possessions as it is to let another have those possessions that he or she desires without hindering that person from taking them. Demanded here is a spirit of both an uncompromising nonretaliation and a radical detachment even from those personal possessions necessary for one's basic human needs.

The next injunction calls for an active response on the part of the disciple, requiring the person not only to give to anyone requesting something but also not to ask for it back. The absolute form of this command "excludes any consideration of the person's background or condition, or the purpose of the begging. Need must not encounter selfish resolve among disciples of the kingdom."[25] Two factors mark the universal scope of this instruction. The present imperative, *didou,* refers to a continual action: "keep giving" (cf. 11:33) over and over again. And, secondly, the recipients of generosity are not limited to one's friends or neighbors, but are to include everyone (*panti*), even one's enemies. An unlimited generosity is called for. No upper limit in terms of frequency can be placed upon a disciple's giving, nor can certain groups or individuals be excluded as recipients of that giving. Furthermore, no restitution is to be sought for what is shared. The motivation for acting in this way is spelled out in verses 32–33. What credit, literally "favor" (*charis*), is there in God's eyes if one loves or does good only to those who can return the favor? What the Lukan Jesus calls for in a few words is unlimited and unrestricted almsgiving. The authority for this radical demand lies in the person of Jesus.

Finally, instructions are given about the practice of lending, first in verse 34: "And if you lend to those from whom you hope to receive, what credit is that to you?" and then in summary form in verse 35, "Lend, expect nothing in return" (literally, "without giving up in despair"). The implied object of "to receive" in verse 34 may be (1) the recovery of the principal (however, one hardly lends without hope of receiving the principal—if so the loan becomes a gift; see 6:30); (2) the payment of interest on the

25Ibid.

loan; or (3) the reception of loans or of some other service in return (cf. vv. 32–33).[26] So it is not clear whether the disciple is being asked to renounce hope of receiving interest, the principal, or a similar favor in return. Envisioned here may well be either a situation where the debtor is an enemy whose animosity is expressed by nonpayment or a situation in which the debtor is too poor financially to be able to repay the loan. In either case, disciples are being asked to lend to others in situations where there will be no personal gain and may even be considerable loss.[27] The "moral economy" envisioned in these verses requires a radical break from the prevailing patron-client relation, wherein some manner of reciprocity would be expected by the client as a way of "repaying" the patron for the benefit given.

The recompense that disciples who act in this way can expect to receive is a "great reward," namely, that they will enjoy the favored status as children of the Most High (6:36). They are given a new corporate identity. Furthermore, by being generous toward the poor they will help to realize God's good news for the poor in concrete ways. This is Jesus' mission; it is the mission of those who follow after him. Nothing less is asked. Thus, disciples are called to be "merciful as your Father is merciful" (6:36).

Those who allow their things to be taken, who give without seeking restitution, and who lend without hope for return—those who act in these ways, often in situations of adversity, are not left unrewarded. This is expressed again succinctly in 6:38: "Give and it shall be given to you." A vivid image is used to dramatize the great generosity that God, the ultimate patron and benefactor, will bestow on the selfless disciple. A good measure running over will be poured out into your lap. Human generosity is rewarded superabundantly by divine generosity.

The privileged place of the poor reaches new heights in Luke's Sermon on the Plain. Only those materially poor, who suffer the pangs of hunger and who have little to laugh about now in their desperate situation, are acclaimed "blessed," because they have a place in God's reign. The present deprivation of the poor is contrasted with future satisfaction. Anyone who now considers him-

---

[26] See Marshall, *Luke*, 263.
[27] See Tannehill, *Unity*, 129–130.

self or herself to be a disciple of Jesus, or anyone from the listening crowd who aspires to be a disciple, is called to act on behalf of the poor, even when the poor may be viewed as one's enemy.

After the Sermon on the Plain, Luke continues the narrative with two healing miracles by Jesus: the cure of a centurion's servant (7:1-10) and the raising of a widow's son (7:11-17). These and other such happenings do not go unnoticed by the disciples of John the Baptist.

F. Jesus' Testimony to John's Disciples (7:18-23)

After John the Baptist is imprisoned, two of his disciples bring word to him about "all these happenings" (7:18) concerning Jesus. Wondering whether Jesus is the expected one, John sends two of his disciples to Jesus to inquire, "Are you 'He who is to come' or are we to expect someone else?" (7:19). Before giving Jesus' reply, the narrator comments: "At that very time Jesus was curing many of their diseases, afflictions, and evil spirits; he also restored sight to many who were blind" (7:21). Hence John's disciples are witnesses to what Jesus is doing, and they can tell John on the basis of their own testimony. Already by this point in the narrative the reader has become informed of the many people Jesus has cured: those with diseases (4:40; 6:19; 7:1-10), those with afflictions (4:38-40; 6:6-11), and those with evil spirits (4:33-37, 41; 6:18). The narrator also states that many blind people have received their sight. However, so far Luke has not reported any specific cures of blind people (as he does later; see 18:35-43), although Jesus has warned about the dangers of blindness in a metaphorical sense (6:39, 41-42) and has given instructions about how to overcome this impairment (6:42).

Having worked many cures, Jesus introduces his verbal response to John's disciples by telling them to report to John "what you have seen and heard" (7:22). The past tense of these two verbs of perception confirms the authenticity of the messengers as witnesses. They have observed what Jesus has done. The verb "to see" links the last of the series of deeds in 7:21 ("to many that were blind he restored sight") with the first of a six-member series in verse 22 ("the blind receive their sight"), and the verb "to hear" points especially to the last member of the series: "The poor have good news preached to them." In a rhythmic series of six short sentences, each with a plural noun and a verb in the present tense, Jesus gives a summary of his activity. In Greek the repetitive pattern gives the words a distinct rhythmic cadence. This joyful cadence of good news has been appropriately called by the German commentator, Hans Schürmann, a "celebration of salvation" (*Heilsjubel*): "The blind see, cripples walk, lepers are cured, the deaf hear, the dead are raised, the poor have received the good news." These saving activities accomplish what has been previously and repeatedly announced in Isaiah[28] and fulfill what is proclaimed by Jesus as his mission in 4:18-19, a text cited from Isaiah. Except for the references to the blind and deaf, the other activities have been previously presented in the narrative: The lame walk (5:12-26); lepers are cleansed (5:17-20); the dead are raised (7:11-17); and the poor have the good news preached to them (6:20). There is no mention of the deaf hearing in the previous summary (7:21), nor is there an account of such in the prior healing activity of Jesus. Similar to what was said about the blind, the possible metaphorical sense of this reference to hearing should not be overlooked. Since the Nazareth scene, Jesus has spent much time preaching, most strikingly in the Sermon on the Plain (6:17-49). To receive these words and to take them seriously requires a "hearing" in the heart that goes far beyond the sensory reception of audible sounds.

By recalling that in biblical literature the first and last members of a series receive the most emphasis, the reader notes that stress falls on the blind seeing and the poor receiving good news. The poor are listed after the blind, lame, and lepers, since disabled persons such as these would generally be poor. To heal those who suffer poverty because of their affliction is indeed to bring good news. There is a further dimension to the lists in 4:18 and 7:22 (as well as to the lists in 14:13 and 21). The lame and the blind are included among those who are blemished in Leviticus 21:18 and hence are forbidden to "draw near to offer up the food of his God" (Lev 21:21). Lepers, too, are ritually unclean (Lev 13–14). Johnson has summarized well the significance of the lists

---

[28]This is not a collection of citations. Instead this is an artful resumé of several texts about the prophecy of salvation: Isaiah 61:1, poor, blind; 29:18-19, deaf, blind, poor; 35:5-6, blind, deaf, lame; 42:18, deaf, blind; 26:19, resurrection of the dead.

just cited: "The unfortunates listed here by Luke are therefore not only weighted with misery; they are rejected from full participation in the life of the people. They are, in a word, the outcasts. But the poor were not considered to be ritually blemished. What is striking is that Luke has included the poor so prominently in each of these lists, as though to assert that in the eyes of men, the poor were just as much in an outcast position, just as rejected from the people, as those with ritual blemish."[29] The radical message of Jesus' proclamation of God's reign, the radical nature of his healing activity, is that it embraces not only "those recognized as belonging to the people, but also, and indeed especially, . . . those on the fringes of the people, the outcasts."[30]

All of these events confirm that the promised time of salvation is at hand. The fulfillment, affirmed in an anticipatory way in 4:21, is now verified on the basis of the words and deeds of Jesus. As recipients of Jesus' saving action, the six classes mentioned here are representative of the oppressed, afflicted classes to whom the message of the Lukan Jesus is brought. Jesus does what he says he was sent to do (4:18-19). The poor are receiving the good news of salvation.

Finally, Jesus tells the disciples of John: "And blessed is the one who takes no offense at me" (7:23). This beatitude reminds the reader that only those who are prepared to accept the offensiveness of Jesus can be called blessed. To accept the coming one unreservedly is to acknowledge, indeed, to serve, those types of folks ministered to by Jesus. So far, many in the Gospel, including Jesus' own townspeople at Nazareth (4:28-30) and the Pharisees (5:21-24, 20, 33-39; 6:1-5), have failed that test and hence cannot, without a genuine conversion, be considered blessed.

G. The Poor Widow (21:1-4)

We began this chapter with the "little people" of the infancy narrative and now conclude with a conspicuous "little person," a poor widow, who is the last of many widows appearing in Luke's narrative (2:36-38; 4:25; 7:11-12; 18:3; 20:47; 21:1-4). In agrarian

---

[29]Johnson, *Function*, 134–135.
[30]Ibid., 134.

societies widows, left to fend for themselves, are especially vulnerable to neglect and exploitation. This widow is observed by Jesus putting into the Temple treasury two copper coins, which represented "all the living that she had" (v. 4). In response to her action Jesus remarks, "Truly I tell you, this poor widow has put in more than all of them; for they all contributed out of their abundance, but she out of her poverty" (vv. 3–4). Usually Jesus' comment is considered to be a word of *praise,* and the widow is extolled as an example of generous giving. However, the meaning of this brief episode may be quite different.

There is a wide range of interpretations advanced for this passage. Five of these follow: (1) The true measure of gifts is not how much is given but how much remains behind; (2) What matters is the *spirit* in which the gift is given and not the amount that is given; (3) The true gift is to give everything one has; (4) Alms and other pious gifts should correspond to one's means; (5) The story expresses the duty of almsgiving.[31] Assuming that the point of the story is to be found in Jesus' saying, one notes that he makes a contrast between the "more" that the widow who has little gives and the gift of those who have an abundance. The sense appears to be that a gift is measured by what is left. Hence, the first interpretation fits the text the best. Nothing is said about the *spirit* of the giver (2) nor about what constitutes a *true* gift (3). And, since the widow has given beyond her means, the fourth explanation does not fit either. Regarding the fifth sense, the story presumes the duty of almsgiving and is, rather, concerned with the degree of giving.

But does the first interpretation, which makes Jesus' comment ("this poor widow has put in more than all the rest") a commonplace observation, give us the deepest significance of the story? Arguing from the context of the story, A. G. Wright suggests that Jesus' comment is actually not a word of *praise* but of *lament.* In the immediately preceding context Jesus calls to task the scribes "who devour widows' houses" (20:47), and in the following passage Jesus speaks about the day to come when the beautifully adorned Temple to which the widow contributes will be torn down

---

[31]See Addison G. Wright, "The Widow's Mite: Praise or Lament?—A Matter of Context," *CBQ* 44 (1982) 256–265, 257–258.

(20:5-6). If Jesus is opposed to devouring widows' houses and if the Temple to which she contributes will soon be destroyed, how can Jesus possibly by pleased by what he sees the widow do? By contributing "all the living that she had" to the Temple treasury, the widow will find it hard to keep her house and will actually be wasting her resources by supporting an institution that will be destroyed. Taking into consideration the context, the reader can conclude that the widow "had been taught and encouraged by religious leaders to donate as she does."[32] Jesus then is saddened by what he sees and condemns the value system that motivates her action as well as those who have conditioned her to do it.

If this interpretation has validity, then the story is a criticism of those who take economic advantage of the religious sensibilities of little people like the poor widow. Such action is reprehensible because it reduces her to a condition of destitution. Although the Lukan Jesus does not praise her, the reader remembers that the victims of such value systems are the ones whom the first beatitude addresses: "Blessed are you poor, for yours is the kingdom of God" (6:20).

Conclusion

Through the first several chapters of Luke's Gospel narrative, one of his central concerns is the privileged place the poor hold in God's eyes, as this is exemplified predominantly in the words and deeds of Jesus. Even those events leading up to and surrounding the birth of Jesus at the beginning of the story are marked by God's preference for "little people" rather than the rich and powerful. God acts to bring forth fruit from the barren womb of Elizabeth and the young handmaid Mary. Emerging as God's spokespersons for the poor are, to some extent, Mary, and to even a lesser extent, John the Baptist; but by far the most significant one is Jesus, called by the heavenly voice the Son of God. In her canticle Mary sounds a theme that will become a familiar refrain throughout the narrative. God *has already* reversed the fortunes of the lowly and the hungry on the one hand and of the rich and

---

[32]Wright, "Widow's Mite," 262. On the exploitation of widows see Douglas E. Oakman, "The Countryside in Luke-Acts," in Jerome Neyrey (ed.), *The Social World of Luke-Acts. Models for Interpretation* (Peabody, Mass.: Hendrickson, 1991) 151–179, 168–169.

the proud on the other hand. The ethical preaching of the Baptist to the crowds, the toll collectors, and the soldiers, if taken to heart, will mean that the hungry will be fed, that the poorly clad will be clothed, and that dishonest practices, which lead some to impoverishment, will be curbed.

The champion of the poor is Jesus. Many readers of the narrative will be convinced that Jesus' main mission is to proclaim the good news of God's reign to the poor. Jesus does this consistently and repeatedly, not only in his preaching but also in his saving deeds. The poor are pronounced blessed, Jesus tells them, for no other reason—need there be any other?—than that theirs is the kingdom of God. A number of times the question has been asked: Who are the poor? A reliable response to this inquiry comes from the narrative context of the various passages that are studied. In Jesus' inaugural discourse, in which he announces that his mission is "to bring glad tidings to the poor," the poor are the debtors, the blind, the captives, and the imprisoned. In the Sermon on the Plain, the poor are the disciples who have left everything voluntarily as well as those from the crowd who have come to follow Jesus. These poor are the hungry, the mourning, and those persecuted. Does this mean that "poor" does not have an economic dimension in the Gospel? Not at all! For those who are imprisoned, those who suffer some infirmity, for example, blindness, and those who are hungry are most often those without financial resources.

Throughout this chapter we have touched upon some of the most radical demands in the Gospel that have been placed upon the disciples of Jesus. For instance, they are to give the possessions they need for their own well being to those who take them. But this is not the only response that disciples of Jesus are called to make. This takes us to the next chapter, in which we will look at the multifaceted relationship between discipleship and possessions.

3

Discipleship and Possessions

In the Gospels, to be a disciple is to be called by Jesus, to follow after him on the journey, and to spend time with him in his way of life. Closely linked with the call to discipleship is the invitation to take part in the mission of Jesus. To be a disciple is to be sent out on mission by Jesus to do those things he himself has been sent to do by God. We begin our discussion on discipleship by noting how Jesus himself is presented in Luke's Gospel, his general pattern of life, and particularly his association with the poor and rich. Then we will turn our attention to the disciples of Jesus, beginning with their call experience and continuing with their mission, concentrating in each instance upon the decisions made and the instructions given about possessions.

The second and most extensive part of this chapter will deal with the teaching of Jesus on possessions found in the long travel narration of Luke's Gospel, beginning with 9:51 when Jesus sets out on the journey for the Holy City and extending to 19:28 when he arrives for his Jerusalem ministry. In this part of the narrative, entire chapters (e.g., 12, 14, 16, and 18) are concerned with the dangers of wealth and the use of possessions. The recipients of this teaching are sometimes the disciples, at other times the crowd, or both together. The passages to be considered will be discussed, as much as possible, following their order in the narrative. Inevitably there will be some repetition of themes. The recurrence of related teachings helps to impress upon the reader the importance that the proper use of possessions has in the Third Gospel.

A. A Portrait of Jesus: Jesus and Poverty

The Gospel portrays Jesus as coming from unpretentious origins, being raised in Nazareth in Galilee (2:4; 4:16), spending his public adult life as an itinerant preacher in the area of Galilee (4:14–9:50), and then setting out on a journey from Galilee to Jerusalem (9:51–19:28), where he is put to death. As we saw at the beginning of the last chapter, Jesus is born in humble circumstances in his ancestral town of Bethlehem, away from his parents' home in Nazareth. Since there is no place for Mary and Joseph inside the village lodgings (2:7), they find an outside place for animals, which serves as an emergency shelter for them, at least for a few days. There Mary gives birth to the family's firstborn son. After his birth Jesus is laid in a *phatnē* (2:7, 16), which can mean either a "stall" to keep animals or a "manger," that is, a feeding trough for domesticated animals. Already, in the circumstances of his birth, Jesus is associated with the homeless. Eight days later Jesus is taken to the Temple in Jerusalem, where his parents offer in sacrifice "a pair of turtledoves, or two young pigeons" on the occasion of his consecration to the Lord (2:24). Two doves or pigeons is the prescribed offering for those who cannot afford the one-year-old lamb for the burnt offering (Lev 12:8). Although this does not tell us a great deal about the socioeconomic situation of Jesus' parents, it does allow us to infer that they are not folks of great or even moderate means.

During his public ministry, having neither a permanent residence nor a supportive occupation, Jesus is frequently on the road, journeying "through cities and villages" (8:1; cf. 13:22), walking the countryside by day, often spending his nights out in the open (6:12). Unlike Mark's Gospel, where Jesus has a regular headquarters at Peter's house in Capernaum, Luke's Gospel portrays a more homeless Jesus. After he and his disciples are turned away by the Samaritans, Jesus vividly describes the kind of life he leads to a would-be follower: "Foxes have holes, and birds of the air have nests; but the Son of Man has nowhere to lay his head" (9:58). This is more than a statement about the lot of a common person in a depressed economy; it is a pronouncement and a warning to would-be disciples about the rejection, persecution, and homelessness they can expect and cautions about the hazards of following such a leader.

Later in Luke's narrative, when Jesus is confronted by his opponents with a trick question about paying tribute, he asks one of them for a coin. The assumption is that Jesus himself does not carry money (20:20-26). As to support for himself and his followers, Jesus relies on others. Luke tells the reader that a group of women who accompany Jesus and his disciples provide for them "out of their means" (8:3). These women make their possessions, monetary and otherwise, available to Jesus along his journey. Another time, Jesus uses Simon's boat on Lake Gennesaret as a place where he sits to teach the people (5:3). Though he himself has little to call his own, Jesus is obviously not adverse to using material things.

Jesus is not a world-renouncing ascetic but one who enjoys the hospitality of others. He is a guest at the house of Simon, a Pharisee (7:36-50); he is received into the home of Martha and Mary (10:38-42); he dines at the house of a ruling Pharisee (14:1-24); he invites himself to Zacchaeus' home, where he is joyfully received (19:1-10); and as risen Lord he breaks bread with two of his disciples (24:28-35). As the story of Jesus with Simon unfolds, Jesus the guest takes on the role of host, first by teaching Simon a lesson about forgiveness and love (7:39-43), then by receiving the woman who comes and anoints the feet of Jesus. In other accounts similar role reversals take place in which "Jesus the guest extends some form of invitation to his hosts or table partners" (see 5:29-39; 10:38-42; 11:27-28; 14:1-24; 19:1-27; 24:13-25).[1] It is Jesus' association with tax collectors and sinners, as both their guest and host, that leads to charges being brought against him (5:29-32) for the type of company he keeps. Furthermore, while Jesus is frequently received by some who offer him hospitality, he is rejected by others who refuse him. For instance, the Samaritan villagers do not receive him (9:51-56), nor do the people of his hometown at Nazareth, where he is found to be unacceptable (4:16-30, esp. v. 24).[2] Such is his poverty. Accepted by some, rejected by others, he continues to proclaim by word and deed the saving presence of the kingdom of God.

---

[1]Koenig, *Hospitality,* 90–91.

[2]On the characteristic Lukan use of "receive" and "not receive" vocabulary (*dechomai* and its compounds), see Tannehill, *Unity,* 235–236.

There is yet another dimension to the poverty of Jesus, a poverty not to be found primarily in his lack of material possessions but rather in his faith.[3] This is poverty at a more theological level. In this vein Paul interprets the poverty of Jesus as his taking on the human condition, as becoming incarnate: "For you know the grace of our Lord Jesus Christ, that though he was rich, yet for your sake he became poor, so that by his poverty you might become rich" (2 Cor 8:9; cf. Phil 2:5-8). Luke presents Jesus as one who has put aside his own self-project in order to pursue God's design for his life. On the night before his death Jesus reaffirms his disposition: "Not my will but yours be done" (22:41). Frequently at prayer (3:21; 4:1, 42; 6:12; 9:28-29; 10:21; 11:1; 22:41) and especially at those times of momentous decisions, he listens to hear God's word made known to him in solitude and in the circumstances of daily life. Turning away from any desires of a personal agenda, Jesus loses his life (cf. 17:33). He lives by his words: "I am in your midst as the one who serves you" (22:27).

B. The Call and Voluntary Poverty of the Disciples (5:1-11, 27-32)

When Jesus calls the first disciples, they leave everything to follow him. When Jesus sends them on mission to collaborate in preaching the good news, he instructs them to take nothing for the journey and to rely instead upon the hospitality of others. Later, at the Last Supper, Jesus somewhat unexpectedly modifies these instructions when he says that greater provisions are now allowed for the journey. How is the total surrender of possessions by the disciples to be interpreted? Is this to be understood as a condition of discipleship only for the time of Jesus or also for Luke's community and later generations of believers? Also, how are we to understand the seemingly new set of instructions to the disciples just before Jesus' death? As one author has put the question, "It was all well and good for Jesus to invite some of his followers to give all to the poor and come follow him, but if Luke's contemporaries were to give all they owned to the poor or to the leadership and if the delay in Jesus' second com-

---

[3] See Johnson, *Sharing,* 74, who comments: "it is in the human faith of Jesus that we find the deepest dimension of poverty."

ing continued, how could their dispossession be prudent?"⁴ These
are some of the questions we have to examine after first looking
at the texts.

The first call story in the Gospel takes place when Jesus encounters Simon and his two business partners, James and John,
who are engaged in their fishing activity (5:1-11). After Jesus gives
Simon a new mission instructing him that from now on he will
be "catching" people instead of fish, Simon and his associates
respond by leaving "everything" (*panta*) and following him (5:11).
Unlike Mark's call stories (1:16-20), those of Luke stress that they
leave behind *everything*. This would include home, family, and
business—all their possessions. The break is complete. The narrative is not clear whether Jesus himself instructs them to leave
everything or whether they do so on their own initiative. Whatever the case, the total surrender of their possessions is not because of some ascetic ideal but because of the call they have
received. They come to believe that "their real life lay not with
what was left behind, but with him who called them forward"
to follow him.⁵ In the call story of 5:1-11 Luke uses for the first
time in the narrative the verb "to follow" (*akoloutheō*, v. 11),
a term for Christian discipleship that occurs frequently in the rest
of the story (5:27-28; 9:23, 49, 57, 59, 61; 18:22, 28). It implies
"an internal attachment and commitment to Jesus and the cause
that he preaches."⁶ By answering the call, the disciples throw in
their lot with Jesus and follow him. For the disciples, Jesus becomes the purse that does not wear out, the purse in which they
invest their treasure (cf. 12:33-34).

Later, during the dramatic encounter between Jesus and the
wealthy ruler, Peter reminds Jesus of the disciples' complete
renunciation: "Lo, we have left our homes and followed
(*ēkolouthēsamen*) you" (18:28). What did this cost them? Johnson remarks: "It does not matter here that the disciples left 'only'
boats and nets and families, whereas the ruler had to leave 'great
wealth.' " Their own things, which they left, were "no less pre-

⁴Haughey, *Money*, 8.
⁵Johnson, *Sharing*, 67–68.
⁶Fitzmyer, *Luke*, I, 569.

cious than the ruler's money. It was no easier leaving them because they were small; in fact it may have been harder."[7]

Closely connected with the call story of the fishermen is that of the tax collector Levi (5:27-32). In response to Jesus' invitation, "Follow me," Levi leaves "everything" (*panta*) behind and goes after him. Thus, he makes a decisive break with his old life and a decision for continued discipleship (cf. the indicative *ēkolouthei* [he followed], v. 28). Then Levi gives a great banquet for Jesus, a large crowd of his fellow tax collectors, and others.[8] Though he is not as wealthy as the chief tax collector, Zacchaeus, Levi is apparently well-to-do, since only those with a large home can afford to give a banquet for a great crowd of guests. The hospitality Levi offers plus the guests he invites prefigures subsequent situations of table fellowship with Jesus, his host, and the guests. Jesus specifies that those invited to dinner should be the poor, the infirm, and the street people (14:13, 21-23).

In the first two call stories Luke accentuates the complete renunciation of possessions as an integral part of the response for those who follow Jesus. It is interesting to note that in these two call episodes Jesus summons no poor people to the circle of disciples, but possessors, those who have something to leave behind. This may reflect that Luke's main concern was for those within and without his community who had possessions.

C. Call and Mission (chs. 9–10)

The disciples' call to be "fishers of people" in 5:10 is realized in the two Lukan missionary narratives, one in chapter 9 about the sending of the Twelve, the other in chapter 10 about the sending of the seventy(-two)[9] to proclaim the reign of God. The second of these narratives shows that the author's interest includes other missionaries in addition to the Twelve. Common to both accounts is Jesus' instruction to take nothing for the journey. In

[7]Johnson, *Sharing*, 67.

[8]Those who point out the inconsistency between first leaving all and then hosting a great banquet identify a tension in the story that was probably not in Luke's mind. The stress is not put on the sequence of events. There is no problem in understanding Levi as leaving all after the banquet.

[9]Some ancient manuscripts read "seventy" (see the RSV); others have "seventy-two" (see the New American Bible).

9:3 the Twelve are to take "no staff, nor bag, nor bread, nor money; and to have two tunics"; and in 10:4 the broader group of disciples are not to carry a staff or a traveling bag, nor are they to wear sandals. Essentially, they are to live the way Jesus lives as they become participants in his mission. Presupposed in these instructions is that the disciples have some resources to draw upon if necessary (cf. 8:1-3); hence they are not completely poverty stricken. This presents a small modification to the complete renunciation that follows their call.

When going out on mission there is no need for them to carry provisions, since they are to rely upon the hospitality of those receiving them. Their hosts are to provide for their daily needs. In 9:4 the Twelve are to stay at whatever house they enter. In 10:5 the disciples, upon entering a house, are instructed to say, "Peace be to this house," and then to stay in the "house eating and drinking what they provide" (v. 7). Missionaries are to expect food and shelter from those who receive their peace greeting and to extend to them hospitality. If they are not received the missionaries are to shake the dust from their feet as a sign of God's judgment upon that particular town (9:5; 10:11; cf. Acts 18:6). In both passages the emphasis is not so much on the poverty of the messengers as such but on their acceptance or rejection by those whom they encounter. The message and the messenger cannot be dissociated; to reject one is to reject the other (cf. 10:16). The theme of opposition and rejection is particularly poignant in the second narrative. For Jesus sends out the seventy-two disciples with the reminder: "I send you out as lambs in the midst of wolves" (10:3).

The sense of hostility intensifies just prior to the death of Jesus. Satan takes possession of Judas, prompting him to plot Jesus' betrayal (22:3); Satan has even asked for all the disciples, to sift them like wheat (22:31). In this context after the Last Supper Jesus recalls and alters his earlier instructions to his disciples. He asks them: " 'When I sent you out with no purse or bag or sandals, did you lack anything?' They said, 'Nothing.' He said to them, 'But now, let him who has a purse take it, and likewise a bag. And let him who has no sword sell his mantle and buy one' " (22:35-36). The disciples' response to Jesus' query indicates that up until now in the narrative their needs were provided for by those who had offered them hospitality. They were accepted by the households of those to whom they preached.[10] But now, just prior to the death of Jesus, the circumstances have changed. The crisis builds, and so it is time for a new set of instructions. Since the opposition to Jesus has been mounting (cf. 11:53-54; 19:47; 20:19), the apostles "must be on their guard and must provide for themselves, for they are part of the crisis."[11] The impending crisis means that Jesus will be reckoned as a transgressor (22:37) and that the disciples will be entering into a situation of intensified persecution, not only at the time around the death of Jesus but afterwards as well. The disciples will now need to take with them a purse for financial support, a traveling bag, sandals, even a sword. The rejection portrayed earlier as an experience of inhospitality (10:1-16) is now understood as an experience of persecution threatening their very lives.

Since 22:35-36 represents a revoking of Jesus' earlier instructions to the disciples (chs. 9 and 10), the reader is led to ask: What does the voluntary complete renunciation of possessions by the disciples in the Gospel of Luke mean? Walter Pilgrim has summarized and evaluated three different interpretations.[12]

1. One explanation assumes that the two different sets of instructions are intended for two different groups. The demand for a total surrender of possessions required by the earthly Jesus for the Twelve and the seventy-two during their missionary activity is directed to the Church leaders in Luke's own community who in effect represent the disciples in the life of Jesus. The argument is that full-time disciples, whether during the life of Jesus or during later periods of the Church, are required to renounce all their possessions. The instructions about the wise use of possessions (see those passages discussed in the rest of this chapter) are intended for the other Christian believers in Luke's community.[13] This interpretation is not convincing, Pilgrim argues, because others besides the Twelve and the seventy-two are also called to abandon their possessions (see 14:33; 12:33; 18:29; 9:57). Com-

---

[10]See Johnson, *Function,* 164.

[11]Fitzmyer, *Luke,* II, 1430.

[12]See Walter Pilgrim, *Good News to the Poor* (Minneapolis: Augsburg, 1981) 98–102.

[13]See, e.g., Degenhardt, *Lukas,* esp. 215–216, who is cited by Pilgrim, *Good News,* 186, n. 18.

plete renunciation in the Lukan narrative is not limited to the Twelve or the seventy-two. Also, in the early chapters of Acts not only the community leaders but all the believers abandon their possessions by sharing them in common. Pilgrim concludes that "the attempt to explain the sayings calling for a total surrender of possessions as something intended only for the apostles and their successors in the early Church fails to match the evidence either in Luke's gospel or Acts."[14]

2. Another group of interpreters holds that Luke writes in a situation in which many Christians "were faced with the loss of their possessions if they publicly confessed loyalty to Christ. Luke meets this threat by underscoring the need to be ready, if necessary, to give up everything for the faith as part of the cost of discipleship."[15] The gist of this argument is that demand for complete renunciation belongs to specific times of crisis and persecution and is not valid for every time and place. Christians who are not threatened with the loss of their possessions are to share them generously with those in need. Pilgrim replies that while it is true that some texts link the problem of possessions with the effects of persecution (see, e.g., 6:20-23; 14:25-33), the demand to leave all is often unrelated to persecution (5:11, 28; 12:33; 14:33; 18:22). Rather, this demand is frequently a response to the call to discipleship in passages where persecution is not a factor.

3. The call to surrender one's possessions is limited for Luke only to the time of the earthly Jesus and his disciples; from the time of the resurrection (or the death of Jesus, cf. 22:35-36), a new form of discipleship is called for. Why, then, all the emphasis on this theme? Luke's intent is "to offer a powerful criticism against wealthy Christians in his own time. By presenting this ideal so forcefully, Luke hopes to spark a dialogue with rich Christians, in which the model of Jesus and the disciples will be the motivating power to the right use of their own wealth."[16] Marshalled in support of this view is 22:35-38, where the Lukan Jesus legitimizes a new form of discipleship in which personal posses-

---

[14]Pilgrim, *Good News,* 99.

[15]Ibid., 100. For this view see, e.g., Walter Schmithals, "Lukas-Evangelist der Armen," *Theologia Viatorum* 12 (1973-74) 160-174, pp. 160-167, as cited from Pilgrim, 186, n. 20.

[16]Pilgrim, *Good News,* 101, holds this view. See also Schottroff and Stegemann, *Hope,* 77-87.

sions may be used and retained. Nonetheless, reflects Pilgrim, who supports this view, "We want to be very cautious lest we create too sharp a separation between the time of Jesus and the time of the church."[17] He remarks that the portrait of the early Church where all things were held in common (Acts 2; 4) is not far from Jesus' radical demand to "sell all and give to the poor."

Of the three alternative explanations sketched by Pilgrim, the third is the most persuasive. The demand for complete renunciation found repeatedly in the Gospel does prompt the sincere reader, including rich Christians, to make decisions about the use of their wealth on the basis of their faith in Christ. Often, this leads the faith-filled believer to share resources generously with those in need. However, one ought not to exclude the validity of the more radical demand for complete renunciation. For example, today the God of Jesus Christ may be calling a few Christians to abandon all possessions as their response to discipleship.

Many contemporary writers frequently use the slogan "option for the poor," which can mean anything from a general concern for the poor to identifying with the poor, depriving oneself for the poor, or actually sharing in the very conditions of the poor. Some disciples will be called to actual poverty. According to one author, "being one of the poor voluntarily is the final stage of the journey or the steepest, narrowest part of this road and the most complete form of obedience."[18] The complete voluntary renunciation of personal possessions and the forgoing of comfortable circumstances in order to share the life of the poor is one radical response to discipleship preserved in the gospel tradition by Luke. In the following chapters of the Lukan narrative the reader is presented with a variety of ways of dealing with possessions. Some of these are models for the correct use of wealth by the believer; they are expressions of generosity and bring life to the community. Other responses are self-serving, leading to the destruction of one's self and harm to the community.

[17]Pilgrim, *Good News,* 101.
[18]Haughey, *Money,* 151.

D. Avoid Greed and Trust in God (ch. 12)

Before coming to chapter 12, where the Lukan Jesus addresses some misguided thinking about possessions, the reader notices the exemplary use of personal possessions in the parable of the Good Samaritan (10:25-37). Jesus instructs an inquisitive lawyer seeking "to inherit everlasting life" (v. 25) about the true manner of being neighbor to such types as a beaten and robbed victim lying alongside the road. A Samaritan who happens to pass by demonstrates genuine neighborliness by his compassion and loving action to this unfortunate stranger. He uses his possessions to help a dying victim. Sometimes referred to as an early paramedic, this Samaritan dresses the man's wounds and pours on some of his oil and wine. Then the Samaritan puts his beast at the service of the victim by taking him to an inn. Once there he pays in full his lodging expenses and offers to cover further costs. At the end of the parable Jesus instructs the lawyer to "go and do the same" (v. 37). The concrete situation of the moment calls forth a faith response to share one's resources. No personal risks are calculated prior to the call to action. No further criteria are weighed about whether to act or about how to use one's possessions except the exigencies of helping a fellow human being.

In chapter 12 Jesus confronts the crowd with some illusory and distorted ways of dealing with possessions. One theme running through this chapter is the misguided search for life's security. One person tries to find it by getting hold of his share of inheritance from his brother (12:13-15); another, a rich farmer, believes that his security can be assured by storing up an abundant harvest (12:16-21). For the disciples, anxieties arise over their concern for the basic necessities of life: food and clothing (12:22-31). According to the faith conviction of Jesus, one's security, or never-failing treasure, is to be found neither by running after things nor by storing up goods but by turning one's heart to the Lord (12:33-34).

After Jesus warns the disciples about the "yeast of the Pharisees," he instructs them about not fearing those who can kill the body and counsels them to testify about him before others (12:1-12). Then someone from the crowd asks Jesus to settle the dispute about the family inheritance (12:13-15). Two people are evidently divided, even antagonistic, over the possession of a piece of property. Jesus, however, showing no interest in the facts of the case, refuses to intervene in the quarrel as an arbitrator. Instead, he goes straight to the heart of the matter, that is, the covetousness that underlies the request and the false evaluation of this human problem in economic terms. Using this as a teaching moment for the crowd, Jesus instructs them to "avoid greed [*pleonexia*] in all its forms" and that one's "possessions do not guarantee . . . life" (12:15). Among its forms, greed would certainly include love of money and the unquenchable desire for ever-greater amounts. It "is a sickness of the soul, which is unable to find rest."[19]

The following parable in the narrative provides a vivid illustration of greed at work and its perilous consequences (12:16-21). The story begins with the introduction of a rich man who has had a good harvest. A harvest is one of the images used for the kingdom of God, but for this rich person, the solitary figure in the story, his harvest becomes his downfall. With no place to store his bumper crop, he asks himself: "What shall I do . . .?" (v. 17; cf. 3:10, 12, 14; 18:18). As we have seen, in Luke's Gospel this is no mundane query but a question of salvation, of life and death. His decision is to build larger grain bins to store his accumulation. Thus he hopes to acquire security for the future and a relaxed lifestyle for the present, when he can eat heartily, drink well, and enjoy himself (12:19). Such eating and drinking in luxury is a negative symbol for the debauchery of "this age," which will be condemned in future judgment (cf. 16:19-31; 17:26-29). His "way of handling his possessions symbolizes his way of treating his life,"[20] so that by storing his excess grain in a secure place, he thinks that his life is secure. The greater his stored-up material goods, the safer he feels about his life.

Notice how isolated this man is in the story. We hear nothing about family, friends, or even enemies. He is closed in upon him-

---

[19] Schottroff and Stegemann, *Hope*, 96. These authors give Plutarch's description of greed as being "like love of money, an insatiable longing for wealth that brings tribulations, troubles, and sleepless nights. Greed drives out such virtues as compassion, kindness to friends, and level headedness, and replaces them with flattery, ambition, and vanity." They add that "elsewhere too in Hellenistic moral exhortation, greed is the vice of vices and one of the more important causes of evil in the world."

[20] Johnson, *Sharing*, 63.

self. His speech betrays his selfishness, for he does not see beyond "my crops," "my barns," "my grain," and "my goods."
His action is not without its social consequences. For in storing
up grain he has, according to some authors, "taken part in an
economic crime that is of major importance in the economy of
antiquity. He has not simply secured his own future in a relatively
harmless way; he has harmed society by holding back his harvests. This is what drives up the price of grain."[21]

Shattering his illusion of security is God's word of judgment:
"Fool! This night your soul is required of you; and the things
you have prepared, whose will they be?" (12:20). He is addressed
as a "fool" not because he has possessions but because he is de-
void of piety toward God, consideration toward his neighbor (cf.
16:19-31), and regard for his true well being. This person seems
to be quite unaware that his life is a gift or loan from God that
must be returned,[22] an idea that may be conveyed by the verb "to
be required of" (*apaitousin*) in verse 20, cited above. Using 12:33
("Sell your possessions, and give alms; provide yourselves with
purses that do not grow old, with a treasure in heaven that does
not fail") as the framework to interpret 12:13-21, the reader un-
derstands that this man is a fool because he does not give alms
to his neighbors in need, thereby transforming his possessions into
never-ending heavenly capital, a never-failing treasure.[23] Finally,
he is a fool because in letting his possessions control his life, he
will come to find out that his life, like his possessions, will also
perish. The story ends with the evaluation that a person who grows
rich selfishly instead of growing rich in the sight of God places
his or her life in peril.

Next Jesus addresses his disciples (12:22-31). Having left all their
possessions, their economic situation is the opposite of that of
the rich farmer. Over against his superabundance is their need.
The disciples are anxious about getting their basic requirements
for food and clothing met. To allay their fears, Jesus uses ordinary examples from nature by referring to how God provides for
the birds, the lilies, and the grass of the fields. In the same way,
Jesus tells them, God "will provide for you, O weak in faith!"

[21]Schottroff and Stegemann, *Hope,* 97.

[22]See Marshall, *Luke,* 524.

[23]See Karris, "Rich and Poor," 120.

(v. 28) if only you will trust in God. Since the disciples live in the new age, the reign of God, they are called to have total dependence on God, to replace their anxiety with trust. "Do not live in fear, little flock. It has pleased your Father to give you the kingdom" (12:32). Then he instructs them: "Sell what you have and give alms. Get purses for yourselves that do not wear out, a never-failing treasure with the Lord which no thief comes near nor any moth destroys. Wherever your treasure lies, there your heart will be" (vv. 33–34). Material resources are to be used by sharing them generously with others in need. One notes that the word "almsgiving" comes from the Greek term *eleēmosunē,* meaning "kind deed," "compassion," "fellow feeling." In time "the compassion that evoked the act became the name of the act itself. So compassion manifested itself in almsgiving."[24] By giving alms, disciples will obtain for themselves a never-failing treasure.

In the rest of chapter 12 Jesus speaks about being prepared for the return of the Master (12:35-59), and in chapter 13 he calls for repentance, works a Sabbath cure, and tells parables about the reign of God.

E. Invite the Uninvited (ch. 14)

The setting for most of chapter 14 takes place with Jesus as a dinner guest at the house of one of the leading Pharisees (v. 1). After Jesus cures a man who suffers from dropsy (vv. 2–6), he instructs his fellow dinner guests in parables that challenge conventional practices of both guests and hosts. Jesus addresses successively the guests as a whole (v. 7), the master of the house (v. 12), and then one of the guests, who speaks out about those who are blessed (v. 15).

In the first parable Jesus calls to task those invited guests who are intent upon getting the places of honor at the table (vv. 7-11). The term used for "place of honor" (*prōtoklisia,* v. 8) literally means "first couch," but it has a broader metaphorical sense and refers to those whose ambition is climbing to the top socially. Such as these, Jesus says, will find their condition reversed, "for every one who exalts himself will be humbled, but the one who humbles

---

[24]Haughey, *Money,* 146.

himself will be exalted" (v. 11). Those who compete for honor bring upon themselves the judgment of eschatological reversal.

The reception extended to Jesus and his fellow guests by the unnamed Pharisee provides an occasion for Jesus to give instructions about offering hospitality (vv. 12–14). The customary practice of the time was for the host to invite his friends or brothers or relatives or wealthy neighbors (v. 12). Having invited people of some means like himself, the host knows very well that according to the practice of reciprocity his favor will be returned. He can expect to be invited back, and thus to be fully repaid. In this way he will have received his consolation now (cf. 6:24), but he may find himself denied God's recompense, as has been made clear to the reader in the Sermon on the Plain.

Jesus offers a new and radical instruction to all hosts: Invite those who cannot repay you, namely, the poor, the maimed, the lame, and the blind (v. 13). These are overlapping social groups on the fringes of society. The poor are those who are blemished and homeless. The sick, unable to work and hence without resources, are also among the poor. The person who becomes a host by extending solidarity to these outsiders is called "blessed" (*makarios*) by Jesus, for "You will be repaid at the resurrection of the just" (v. 14).

This word of blessing elicits a rejoinder by another member of the Pharisee's dinner party, who seems to "correct" Jesus by saying: "Blessed is he who shall eat bread in the kingdom of God" (v. 15).[25] In other words, this person seems to be saying, "It is not settled that they who invite the poor and other beggars to table will be rewarded at the resurrection of the just; let us therefore say that they are to be called blessed who will in fact share in the banquet in the kingdom of God."[26] To this Jesus responds with another banquet parable, which warns his "corrector" and anyone present from concluding too quickly that he or she can count on being present for the messianic banquet.

This parable tells about a person wealthy enough to host a large dinner for invited guests who are also well-situated economically (vv. 16–24). One invitee could afford to buy ten oxen, another

---

[25]Cf. 11:27-28, where the second makarism, spoken by Jesus, "corrects" the first, spoken by the woman.

[26]Schottroff and Stegemann, *Hope*, 100.

to purchase a field. Usually one would welcome such a banquet invitation, since the rich person was in a position to extend favors to the guests. Their business concerns, however, are more important than responding to an invitation to the kingdom of God. These two and a third invited guest are too tied down by their possessions and domestic life to be able to participate in the banquet. Hence, the host sends out his servants twice, once "to the streets and lanes of the city [to] bring in the poor and maimed and blind and lame" (v. 21), and a second time "to the highways and hedges" to compel those there to come fill the banquet room (v. 23). The host in this parable, albeit in a second effort, fulfills the demands of Jesus' teaching just given to invite those who "cannot repay you" (v. 14). The rich and propertied members of Luke's community were to extend hospitality to the poor, to treat them as friends.[27]

The scene changes in verse 25 to another occasion when Jesus, accompanied by a great crowd, begins to teach them about the demands of discipleship. This teaching is capsulized in three all-inclusive conditional sentences, each concluding with the identical phrase, "cannot be my disciple" (*ou dunatai einai mou mathētēs*), which functions to unify this section (vv. 26, 27, 33). The first condition in order to become a disciple is to "hate" father, mother, wife, children, brothers, sisters, indeed one's very self (v. 26). Here, the Lukan Jesus is using parabolic language to stress the radical call of discipleship. The term "hate" is not intended to suggest a strong emotional rejection of the disciple's family but rather means that old loyalties are to be left behind. The final loyalty to be rejected, "even his own life" (*tēn psychēn heautou*), suggests that martyrdom itself may be required of the disciple of Jesus. Recall that at this point in the narrative Jesus is on the road to Jerusalem where he will be put to death; nothing less is expected of the disciple of Jesus. The second conditional sentence explicitly identifies the necessity of taking up one's cross (v. 27). This may mean facing death as a faithful disciple or accepting whatever suffering that is encountered along the journey.

After the cross Jesus addresses the cost of discipleship in terms of one's possessions. The brief tableaux of a person building a

---

[27]Cf. Karris, "Rich and Poor," 121.

tower (vv. 28–30) and a king going to war (vv. 31–32) warn the believer to consider seriously the cost before beginning. Jesus' message is clear: If you cannot see it through to the end, do not begin. The third and climactic conditional sentence of this section lays down the requirement to abandon one's possessions: "So therefore, whoever of you does not renounce all that he has cannot be my disciple" (v. 33). The supreme example of the cost of discipleship is not martyrdom, as might be expected, but the renunciation of possessions. This indicates how important the "problem" of possessions must have been in Luke's community. In light of verses 26–27, the term *hyparchonta* in v. 33, which is usually translated "possessions," may be more inclusive, meaning all that a person has, including family, even one's life.

Again, it is debated whether this last demand is a requirement only for the full-time disciples of Jesus or for all Christians. Or does this mean that a person should be ready to abandon one's possessions if the occasion should require it? A complete surrender for all Christians does not seem to be intended, since the previous instruction in this chapter implies that members of Luke's community had the means to give festive meals for others. Still, the demand for complete renunciation may be required for some disciples by the God who calls them.

F. Using Mammon and "Seeing" the Poor (ch. 16)

After chapter 14, the Lukan Jesus defends himself in the next chapter against the Pharisees and scribes for the company he keeps with sinners and tax collectors (15:1-2). He tells two brief parables, about the lost sheep (15:3-7) and the lost coin (15:8-10), then the dramatic story about the man with two sons (15:11-32). Throughout these stories the deep joy that accompanies the experience of forgiveness radiates in heaven before God and the angels and on earth within the human community (15:6, 7, 10, 24, 32). The theme of possessions plays a supporting role. The shepherd's flock of a hundred sheep and the woman's ten silver coins have an illustrative function. The reclaiming of the lost sheep or the lost coin shows how important it is that the "lost" sinner repent and return to the community. In the story of the man with two sons, the younger son goes out and squanders or misuses his share of the family property. Having dissipated his possessions by self-indulgence, he then diminishes himself to the point that he is less well off than the pigs. On the son's return his father offers him some of the family's most precious possessions, thereby symbolizing the great joy at his son's return. In this moving story, possessions shared dramatize the reconciliation between father and son, and on the level of interpretation, between God and a repentant sinner.

In chapter 16, the narrator places contrasting attitudes toward possessions on center stage and offers evaluative comments. The narrative in this chapter is directed specifically to the disciples (16:1), but within the audience are the Pharisees who hear what Jesus has to say (16:14). The two stories he tells begin in the same way: "There was a rich man . . ." (vv. 1, 19). Already, with these few words of introduction, a rather negative response would be evoked in the first-century reader. It was commonly assumed that a rich person in the ancient Mediterranean world was "either unjust or the heir of an unjust person."[28] The first story is about a rich person and his "unjust" steward; the second is about a rich man and a poor beggar named Lazarus.

In the first story, where it is assumed that the wealthy master's riches have been acquired through oppression or evildoing, the focus of attention is on the activity of his steward, who acts shrewdly when faced with a crisis (16:1-13). After the master charges his steward with wasting his goods, the steward discounts his master's accounts in order to make sure "that people will receive me into their houses when I am put out of the stewardship" (v. 4). For acting so wisely in the face of dire circumstances, the master surprisingly offers a word of praise for the steward (v. 8a). Hence, the master forfeits the "power of tyranny" he has over the readers who, because he is a rich man, initially would view him in a negative light. After his word of praise, the master comes across more favorably.[29] There is thus apparently a place in the reign of God for the rich person who does not act ruthlessly.

What about the steward? At the end of the story there is a stigma attached to him; he is referred to as *adikias* ("unrighteous"), translated as "dishonest" by the RSV (v. 8a). Whether

---

[28]Malina, "Wealth and Poverty," 363. See ch. 1, pp. 30-31.

[29]See B. Brandon Scott, "A Master's Praise: Luke 16, 1-8a," *Biblica* 64 (1983) 173-188, p. 188.

this steward has been thus characterized because of his original mismanagement and profiteering or because he was an accomplice in the wealthy master's bidding is unclear. Whatever the case, the steward's action merits the commendation of the master. By canceling part of their debts the steward relieves the downtrodden, even though there is a selfish dimension to his motivation. Furthermore, the steward in his need reaches out to the human community, perhaps for the first time. He has aided the debtors and thus has made friends with them by returning to them a portion of the material resources he has at his disposal. Once released from his managerial position, the steward will be relying upon their hospitality. This "middle manager" has come to realize that his wealth is in the members of the community rather than in his money. According to one author, "Luke goes another step and intimates a connection between their homes [v. 4] and the manager's eternal dwelling place [v. 9]. From the context of Luke's Gospel one can surmise that the reception of the manager by the community whom he has first bilked and then needed probably refers to the acceptance of pagans into the Christian community."[30]

At the conclusion of the parable (16:8-13) there are a series of interrelated applications and explanations connected by catchwords: acting shrewdly (vv. 8a, 8b), unrighteousness (*adikia*) (vv. 8a, 9, 10; cf. dishonesty, *adikos,* in v. 10), and mammon (vv. 9, 13). The expressions "make friends for yourselves by means of unrighteous mammon" (v. 9), "he who is faithful in a very little is faithful also in much" (v. 10; cf. vv. 11–12), and "you cannot serve God and mammon" (v. 13) are "different ways of speaking of the same behavior: not holding onto wealth but giving it to those in need."[31] The concluding statement, "You cannot serve God and mammon," is based on the conviction that each of these is an absolute master claiming total loyalty. A person will hate one and love the other. The price of trying to serve both is that of "splitting one's consciousness," creating what one author refers to as "mammon illness."[32] Jesus names the phenomenon and denies that such divided allegiance will work.

[30]Haughey, *Money,* 27.

[31]Tannehill, *Unity,* 131.

[32]See Haughey, *Money,* 14–15.

A specific example of the split-consciousness approach is given in the next few verses (16:14-15). Attention is drawn to the Pharisees, who attempt to justify themselves before God and the people yet are actually "lovers of money" (*philarguroi*). In Luke's narrative, the Pharisees are well enough off to host banquets (7:36; 11:37; 14:1) and are frequently presented as giving more attention to external appearances than to the intentions of their heart. They are concerned to cleanse the outside of eating utensils, but inside they "are full of extortion and wickedness" (11:39); they pay tithes while neglecting the justice of God (11:42); they pride themselves on being righteous and superior to others in religious observance, yet their trust is in themselves rather than in God (18:9-14). Although they try to serve successfully two masters, God and mammon, the Lukan Jesus calls them on their game: "You are those who justify yourselves before people, but God knows your hearts; for what is exalted among others is an abomination in the sight of God" (16:15). By acting in this way, the Pharisees are set in contrast to the "unjust" steward of the preceding parable, who acts shrewdly with the possessions under his control to benefit others even though his motivation is prompted partially by self-interest.

The second parable in this chapter is about a certain rich man and a poor man named Lazarus (16:19-31). The socioeconomic conditions of these two people are drawn in sharp contrast. The rich man is luxuriously clothed; he "feasted sumptuously every day" (v. 19; cf. 1:53; 6:24), while Lazarus "desired to be fed" (v. 20). The rich man fits the description of those referred to earlier in the narrative "who are gorgeously appareled and live in luxury" (7:25). Such people live in courts, usually isolated from others, although this man does have a family of five brothers (16:28). Then there is Lazarus (the only person named in the parables) who is presented as poor (*ptōchos*), sick with a body full of sores, hungry, "unclean" from the dogs who lick his sores, and evidently without family ties (cf. 1:53; 6:20-21; 14:21, 23). Together the rich man and Lazarus are a graphic reflection of the contrasts drawn in the Beatitudes and woes. Although Lazarus is very near the banquet table, the rich man's wealth has inoculated him from any feeling of compassion. The rich man effectively renders Lazarus invisible.

After death their fortunes are reversed. Lazarus is taken to Abraham's bosom, a symbol for participation in the heavenly banquet; the rich man is sent to Hades, where he suffers torment. Now, the rich man, who could not bring himself to touch Lazarus on earth, calls out for Lazarus to alleviate his anguish by touching his lips with his finger. However, the abyss separating them cannot be crossed; it is absolute and eternal. "Because of his chosen inactivity in time, the rich man is deprived of what could have saved him, the sacrament of the poor man's touch. Without it he was inured within the reign of material wealth and all that it procured for him. His comfort and wealth numbed him to the discomfort and grave need of the other which he could have alleviated."[33] The point is clear: The failure to use one's wealth in this life for the poor leads to torment in the afterlife, whereas the poor in this life will be satisfied. "Blessed are you poor, for yours is the kingdom of God" (6:20).

In the second part of the parable, when the rich man asks that his brothers be warned, Abraham reminds him that they have Moses and the Prophets (16:29-31; cf. 16:16-17). It is to his peril that the rich man ignores the Law and the Prophets by refusing to help the poor person in his midst (see, e.g., Deut 15:4). This parable makes clear that the Law is still in force, particularly that portion about responding to the poor.

G. *Quest for Eternal Life* (ch. 18)

In chapters 17 and 18 Jesus continues to teach his disciples, to call them to a deeper faith, and to invite others to the demanding life of discipleship. He does this as the journey draws ever closer to Jerusalem. The narrator tells us that Jesus is "on the way to Jerusalem" (17:11) as he meets ten lepers upon entering a village. Later Jesus himself makes this very plain to the Twelve: "Behold, we are going up to Jerusalem" (18:31). Though they do not understand, Jesus teaches them that in this Holy City the Son of Man does not cling to what he possesses, namely his life, in order to bring about the reign of God. Jesus is willing to surrender what is most precious to him so that God's purposes announced "by the prophets will be accomplished" (18:31).

[33]Haughey, *Money*, 13.

In the course of his teaching to the disciples (17:1) the Pharisees ask Jesus when the kingdom of God is coming (17:20). After telling them that the kingdom is "in the midst of you" (17:21), he instructs them about the future coming of the Son of Man. This will occur at a time when people are engaged in the regular activities of daily life: eating and drinking, buying and selling, planting and building, the same activities that occupied Lot and his family when God's judgment brought destruction to Sodom. Jesus warns his listeners to be indifferent to worldly things on that day. "Let him who is on the housetop, with his goods in the house, not come down to take them away; and likewise let him who is in the field not turn back" (17:31). The disciples are not to allow the seductive power of possessions to prevent them from being completely ready for and instantly receptive to the Son of Man when he comes. At his coming there will be no time, indeed, there will be no point in recovering one's earthly possessions.

Jesus offers the negative example of Lot's wife, who failed the test. Trapped by the alluring power of her possessions, she lingered and lost. As Johnson comments, "Lot's wife . . . was tragically confused. She identified her *being* with her *having,* her life with her possessions. She could not respond to God's call, and so lost the life that she sought to establish by what she owned."[34] The sharp and paradoxical nature of Jesus' teaching is clear: "Whoever seeks to gain [*peripoiēsasthai*] his life will lose it, but whoever loses his life will preserve it" (17:33; cf. 9:24). The verb *peripoieō* means "to acquire, gain for oneself, or possess." Luke's point is that whoever tries to cling to one's life as a possession will end up by losing it. "The irony is that the loss comes not as the result of external punishment, but in the act of grasping itself. Life which comes from God cannot be seized and clung to as though it were ours."[35]

In chapter 18 there are two episodes, one a parable about a Pharisee and a tax collector (18:9-14) and the other a personal encounter between Jesus and a rich ruler (18:18-30), in which attachment to one's possessions becomes a hindrance to authentic life with God. In the first parable the Pharisee boasts about

[34]Johnson, *Sharing,* 62.

[35]*Ibid.*

his religious accomplishments, telling how he exceeds what is required of him: "I fast twice a week, I give tithes of all that I get" (18:12). He clings to his own pious practices as "possessions," believing that these afford him security against the judgment of God. His own religious acts become idols. His professed gratitude to God is actually self-congratulations for his superior position, artificially buttressed by his condescending judgment of others. His true inner attitude is exposed by the narrator from the outset, who says that the parable is addressed to those who believe in their own self-righteousness while holding everyone else in contempt (v. 9). This Pharisee trusts in himself and despises others, while authentic faith is found in the most unlikely of characters, a tax collector. He trusted in God and not in himself; he hopes for what he might receive—God's mercy. The rub in this parable comes at the end with the reversal of status for these two. The Pharisee who claims to be righteous goes home unrighteous; the tax collector who presents himself as a sinner in need of mercy goes home justified. "For every one who exalts himself will be humbled, and the one who humbles himself will be exalted" (18:14).

The second episode in chapter 18 is about the quest of a rich ruler for eternal life (vv. 18–30). Ultimately, this wealthy man fails to obtain his heart's desire because his heart is dominated by material things. Setting this passage in relief are the texts that precede and follow it. Preceding it is Jesus' encounter with children, who symbolize the *anawim,* the poor in spirit or lowly in the community (vv. 15–17). In the words of Jesus, "To such belongs the kingdom of God" (v. 16). Because they have an attitude of humility, like that of the tax collector in the preceding parable, they will enter the kingdom of God. Contrasted to these children, who know nothing of power and wealth, is the ruler who lays claim to both. The other framing passage to the story of the rich ruler is Jesus' prediction of the manner in which he will surrender his very life (vv. 31–34). Childlike simplicity and utter abandonment are the necessary qualities conducive to life in the kingdom of God. Is it possible for a person of wealth to dispose his heart and to dispossess his riches in order to attain the kingdom? Jesus' encounter with the rich man is a test case.

Only in Luke's account is the man with a quest called a "ruler" (*archōn,* v. 18) who is "very rich" (*plousios sphodra,* v. 23; cf. Mark 10:17-31). It seems that Luke intentionally heightened the man's socioeconomic status, perhaps because there were high-ranking and wealthy individuals of his generation who were sincerely interested in following the Christian Way. The question posed by the ruler, "Good Teacher, what shall I do to inherit eternal life?" (v. 18), ought to be taken at face value as a sincere inquiry. Building his case for meriting eternal life, this man affirms that he has kept all the commandments that Jesus cites. However, Jesus calls for a more radical response: "Sell all (*panta*) that you have and distribute to the poor, and you will have treasure in heaven; and come, follow me" (v. 22). Complete renunciation of possessions is required (the addition of *panta* by Luke is not accidental; cf. 5:11, 28). To this requirement is joined two other commands. First, give to the poor (*ptōchoi*). The poor need what others possess in order to have their basic requirements for life fulfilled. Such giving creates solidarity in the community and provides the basis for a new social order. Such giving leads one to realize that material possessions fail as ultimate values in themselves and become "false" treasures, which lure one away from the lasting and "true" treasure in heaven (cf. 12:21, 32-33). The second command is one of discipleship. In the Lukan narrative, renunciation of possessions is a necessary and important step leading to fellowship with Jesus (cf. 5:11, 28). As Tannehill comments, "This is not the achievement of a few outstanding followers, but a requirement of discipleship (at least in the time of Jesus), as Jesus made clear in 14:33."[36]

Rather than heeding the call of Jesus, the rich man becomes sad. For his heart is too firmly captured by his possessions to let go and take up the invitation of Jesus. The rich ruler is a good example of "norm obedience," which falls short of the radical obedience to God. The rich man has attempted to worship God and mammon simultaneously, but when put to the test, it becomes clear that his wealth is really his master.[37] So he fails to obtain his quest for eternal life. Yet this encounter teaches him some-

---

[36]Tannehill, *Unity,* 121.

[37]See the comment by E. E. Ellis, *The Gospel of Luke,* Century Bible (London: Nelson, 1966; 2nd. ed., London: Oliphants, 1974) 217: "Jesus always requires from one just that earthly security upon which one would lean."

thing he didn't know before. He is an idolater. Hence, while he may have kept the second half of the Decalogue, he has not really kept the first and greatest commandment, requiring complete trust in God and self-giving love for the neighbor, encountered in the poor (cf. 10:27).

Unlike the story in Mark, in Luke's Gospel the rich man stays around to hear the reply by Jesus followed by reactions from the crowd and from Peter (18:24-30). Jesus addresses the rich man, saying: "How hard it is for those who have riches to enter the kingdom of God! For it is easier for a camel to go through the eye of a needle than for a rich person to enter the kingdom of God" (vv. 24–25). With this as a word of warning, the discussion is broadened from that of full-time discipleship with Jesus to the problem of wealth for all who seek the kingdom of God. Jesus illustrates the difficulty of entering the kingdom with a hyperbolic expression about a camel, Palestine's largest animal, trying to get through the smallest of known openings, the eye of a needle. Both "camel" and "eye of a needle" are to be taken literally.[38]

To the reaction of the astonished crowd, "Then who can be saved?" (v. 26), Jesus offers a theological reflection: "What is impossible with people, is possible with God" (v. 27). The power of riches to enslave their owners is so great that only strength coming from God enables a person to let go and become a disciple. The point of the camel saying is "not that a few rich people get in with their wealth intact, but that only a few, by a miracle of God," will accept the strength to abandon their bondage to possessions and will place their trust in God.[39] For those with riches who become disheartened by the severity of the camel saying, the path for hope is radical trust in the liberating power of God.

As a spokesperson for the disciples, Peter says that they have already fulfilled the demand made upon the rich man: "We have left homes and followed you" (v. 28). Jesus then expands upon what they have left behind to include their homes and every relationship (wife, brothers, parents, children) and promises them that

[38]See Fitzmyer, *Luke*, II, 1204; Robert H. Stein, *Difficult Sayings in the Gospels: Jesus' Use of Overstatement and Hyperbole* (Grand Rapids: Baker, 1985) 29.

[39]Pilgrim, *Good News*, 121.

they will "receive manifold more in this time, and in the age to come eternal life" (v. 30). People who give everything to God including the most valued earthly security will receive back "many times as much," perhaps meaning a new family in the Christian community (cf. 8:21) as well as the necessities for their daily life (cf. Acts 2:44-45; 4:32-35). Furthermore, they will receive what the rich man sought but failed to gain, eternal life. This is "treasure in heaven" (v. 22). To the readers of Luke's Gospel, the disciples are witnesses that riches can be abandoned and the quest for eternal life attained.

H. Salvation Comes to Zacchaeus (ch. 19)

Luke concludes the travel narrative with the story of Jesus' encounter with Zacchaeus (19:1-10), followed by the parable of the pounds (19:11-27). This brings to a close the whole of Jesus' ministry in Galilee and Judea and leads up to his rejection, suffering, and death in Jerusalem. The Zacchaeus episode is one of Luke's most significant texts on the right use of possessions and hence becomes an example par excellence for rich Christians in the Lukan community. Unlike the rich man in the previous chapter, Zacchaeus responds generously and joyfully to Jesus; he demonstrates the fruit of repentance and receives salvation.

Zacchaeus is presented as a chief tax collector, which means that he was probably the district manager responsible for collecting taxes for a geographical area with assistant tax collectors working under him. By adding that he was rich, Luke reinforces his economic status. This initial presentation of a rich man who was an outsider religiously and socially (part of the non-elite) was likely to evoke a negative reaction among Luke's readers. However, a more sympathetic involvement comes as a fuller picture of Zacchaeus unfolds in the story. This individual is short of stature, is eager to see Jesus, but is hindered from this quest by the crowd. Using his ingenuity to overcome this limitation, he runs ahead along the anticipated route and climbs a sycamore tree so that he can present himself to Jesus. Upon noticing him, Jesus speaks with divine necessity: "I *must* stay at your house today" (v. 5). Jesus prevails upon him to offer him hospitality; Zacchaeus obliges joyfully (contrast the *sad* countenance of the rich man in

18:23). But the crowd raises an objection that has become a familiar complaint at this point about the company Jesus keeps: "He has gone in to be the guest of a man who is a sinner" (v. 7; cf. 5:30).

Then Zacchaeus defends himself by stating that he has been giving alms generously to the poor: "Behold, Lord, the half of my goods I give to the poor" (v. 8). The present tense verb "I give away" (*didōmi*) is to be understood as indicating customary action.[40] If one is to assume with the crowd that Zacchaeus was a sinner,[41] then he has indeed demonstrated the fruits of repentance (cf. 3:10-14). Besides almsgiving, Zacchaeus states his intention to repay fourfold anyone he has defrauded.[42] As a result of this generous almsgiving and manifold reimbursement of funds, Zacchaeus will be left in pretty much the same financial condition required for others, including the disciples and the rich ruler. So it is misleading to think that Zacchaeus is getting by more cheaply.[43] Notice that there is no reference to anything left over.

In response to the crowd's accusation and to Zacchaeus' change of heart by which he is freed from the captive hold of possessions, Jesus offers him salvation *today,* a key term in Luke's Gospel (cf. 2:11; 4:21; 23:43). Furthermore, Jesus confers upon Zacchaeus true membership in the Jewish people by calling him a "son of Abraham" (cf. 1:54-55, 68-75). The story concludes with a summary of Jesus' mission: "For the Son of Man came to seek and to save the lost" (v. 10). What began as a quest by Zacchaeus to see Jesus is transposed at the end into a quest by Jesus to seek out and save. What was thought to be humanly impossible is made possible by the presence of Jesus. Zacchaeus is one shining example of a person with a camel-size wealth who

---

[40]See Fitzmyer, *Luke,* II, 1225.

[41]Even though "all" claim that Zacchaeus is a sinner, this is not at all certain. He does not ask Jesus for mercy, nor does Jesus pronounce forgiveness or speak about his conversion or repentance. See Fitzmyer, *Luke,* II, 1220–1221.

[42]The verb *sykophanteō* is translated "accuse falsely for gain" by A. J. Kerr, "Zacchaeus's Decision to Make Fourfold Restitution," *Expository Times* 98 (1986) 68–71. Kerr suggests that a fourfold penalty in cases where a tax collector brought a false accusation was required by Roman law in Judea.

[43]See Tannehill, *Unity,* 123.

disperses most, if not all, of his riches and thus gets through the needle's eye.[44]

In the following parable of pounds (19:11-27) Jesus warns against an overrealized eschatology (v. 11), instructs the disciples to be accountable to the nobleman who represents Jesus in Luke's narrative, and prepares his followers for his imminent rejection (vv. 14, 27). In this parable, which has been allegorized in Luke, a unit of monetary exchange, the "pound," is used for illustrative purposes. The nobleman gives to the servants "pounds" in varying amounts as a free gift. He charges them to "trade with these till I come" (v. 13). Upon his return he calls the servants to find out "what they had gained by trading" (v. 15). The first two servants are rewarded for the profits they had gained, but the third, who earned nothing, is subject to the nobleman's wrath. He is taught a belated lesson in investment: "Why then did you not put my money into the bank, and at my coming I should have collected it with interest?" (v. 23), and then has his one pound taken away and given to the one who has ten. The "pounds" represent gifts, whether spiritual or material, and are entrusted by Jesus to the Church of Luke's day to be used for the increased benefit of the community. Those who do so will be rewarded with even more; those who do not will lose even what they have (cf. v. 26).

After the long journey of discipleship teaching, Jesus arrives for his Jerusalem ministry, his death, and resurrection (19:28-24:53). His teaching about money matters continues. Arriving at the Temple, the central religious institution for the people Israel, he "began to drive out those who sold" because they have made it a "den of robbers" (19:45-46). Financial corruption has afflicted the officials in the "house of prayer," who are involved in changing foreign currency at a profit, selling animals for sacrifice, and collecting the Temple tax. If economic injustice prevailed here, at the highest level of the religious institutions, it is undoubt-

---

[44]For a recent study of the Zacchaeus story as a quest story, see Robert F. O'Toole, "The Literary Form of Luke 19:1-10," *JBL* 110 (1991) 107-116. For a comparison of similarities between the Zacchaeus story and the call story of Levi in 5:27-32, see Talbert, *Luke,* 176: "In both Jesus is going somewhere; there is a tax collector; Jesus issues an invitation; a positive response is given; Jesus then enters the tax collector's house; an objection is brought; Jesus responds, justifying his behavior; an 'I came' saying is appended."

edly entwined throughout most levels of social life in Israel. Many instances of this do not escape Jesus' notice, as several of his parables and teachings earlier in the Gospel attest. A second scene from the Temple area involving Jesus' observations about a poor widow (20:1-4) was discussed in chapter 1. As we commented, this widow, like those other people cheated by the Temple traders, is probably a victim of religious officials who prompt her to give away all that she has to live on.

Conclusion

We began our discussion of the relationship between discipleship and possessions by looking to the portrait of Jesus in the Gospel. One expects a correspondence in both attitude and action between Master and disciples. The fidelity of the disciples to the Master can be measured by the extent to which they emulate his words and deeds. This, of course, does not require a slavish imitation of the details of his life circumstances nor of his every action. The connection is to be sought rather at the much deeper level of fundamental convictions.

The portrait of Jesus in the Gospel reveals a person who is born and grows up in humble circumstances. During his public ministry he is an itinerant preacher without a permanent place to call his home. The narrative is silent about whether Jesus has his own personal possessions, property, or financial resources. Whatever the case, Jesus is no world-renouncing ascetic who eschews the use of possessions or the enjoyment of the good things of this earth. Numerous times Jesus is a dinner guest of hosts from a wide spectrum of society. In this respect, Jesus neither shuns the rich nor avoids the poor. On the contrary, he instructs his host to invite the street people, the poor, the sick, the blind, who cannot reciprocate. Share your banquet table, Jesus urges, extend your hospitality to those who are without food and drink or a nourishing community. For Jesus himself perhaps the deepest level of his poverty is not the lack of material possessions but his radical trust in God. He is not anxious about acquiring material things, securing life's necessities, or even preserving his own life. He puts aside his own personal agenda, his false self. His faith in God sustains him.

As a teacher Jesus addresses others several times about the danger of possessions. He teaches that the stockpiling efforts of folks like the rich farmer do not provide the security that is so desired. Selfishly holding on to material things isolates a person from the community, as it does this farmer and the rich man in the story about Lazarus. The seductive power of possessions is so strong that it can enslave their owners and turn possessions into idols. Jesus warns that no person can serve two masters at the same time, professing faith in God and giving allegiance to material things. Wealth can be an obstacle to discipleship, as it is for the rich ruler. The seductive power of the world's goods is so strong that Luke places the demand to renounce one's possessions in an emphatic position after that of taking up one's cross, an image suggesting martyrdom.

The instruction Jesus offers to those with possessions cannot be reduced to one concrete mode of action for everyone. In the call stories the disciples abandon *everything* to follow Jesus. Others, such as the rich ruler, are told to do likewise. Such radical demands, not required for all those Jesus encounters, would at least serve to unsettle the consciences of rich Christians, prompting them to share more generously. Some even today may be called to make the same radical response as did the disciples, that is, to renounce everything and thus to share in the very life of the poor. Jesus invites others to give alms to the poor, as Zacchaeus did bountifully. He also instructs his listeners to extend hospitality, especially to the dispossessed and disabled. Common to all these responses is the appeal to break the oppressive bonds of patron-client relations, to create a new social situation in which the basic needs of all are satisfied. Common to all these responses is the mandate to share with others, since everything that a person has is ultimately a gift from the Creator. The response of the believer is to share what has been received as a gift with those who are deprived of such benefits. For no one has an absolute right to the things of this earth. The practice of sharing generously is exemplified in the early Church, whose story Luke tells in Acts, the second part of his narrative. This takes us to the next chapter.

4

Possessions in the Story of the Early Church

In Luke's story of the early Church in Acts the theme of possessions is present, though in a less prominent way than in the Gospel. The most well-known passages are those about the group of believers sharing all things in common in the early chapters of Acts (2:43-47; 4:32-35). Noticeably absent in Acts is any mention of the poor (*ptōchos*), a term frequently occurring in the Gospel.[1] Is this significant? Does this mean that Luke deliberately omits all references to the "poor" from his sources, or that the sources have no reference to such? Luke's silence about the poor is coherent with his portrayal of the Jerusalem community: "There was not a needy person among them" (4:34). Later in the narrative this is no longer the case, as is attested by the famine that hits Judea, prompting a collection to be taken up for the believers who live there (11:27-30).

If the poor do not have a prominent place in the Acts narrative, the rich do. Repeatedly Luke refers to wealthy and influential persons who either join the Way or who are interested in it. As we remarked in the first chapter, one of Luke's apologetic concerns is to show that the Christian movement was attracting individuals well placed from social, political, and economic perspectives.[2] Examples are Lydia the business woman (16:14-15, 40) and the proconsular governor Sergius Paulus (13:4-12). Luke's

[1]See Luke 4:18; 6:20; 7:22; 14:13, 21; 16:20, 22; 18:22; 19:8; 21:3. See above, pp. 51–52.

[2]See ch. 1 above, pp. 25–26.

concern to show that Christianity was gaining credence with the well off and powerful does not prevent him from identifying instances where money is misused and where the power that it affords perverts religious matters. The latter is true, for instance, with Simon the magician (8:11-18) and Demetrius the silversmith (19:23-27).

The proper use of material resources is demonstrated in the early community, where all things are shared in common, and in the giving of alms, referred to on several occasions in Acts. Also, numerous times believers who are heads of households extend hospitality to fellow believers. Paul, in particular, is frequently a recipient of hospitality, though he also demonstrates his self-sufficiency.

This chapter will begin by tracing Luke's portrayal of the early community, which shares all things in common, and of the unraveling of this shared vision. Then we will discuss the texts relating to almsgiving and the collections and follow with a presentation of episodes where money is misused. Finally, the theme of hospitality will be highlighted.

A. Sharing All Things in Common: Success and Failure (chs. 2–6)

The beginning of Acts is a story of the Spirit. The Holy Spirit is promised on the occasion of the Lord's ascension (1:8) and is received in fullness at Pentecost by many believers from places near and far (2:1-13). After Peter's sermon to representatives of Judaism from all over the world gathered in Jerusalem, the crowd asks him and the rest of the apostles, "What shall we do?" (2:37; cf. Luke 3:10-14). Peter calls upon them to repent, be baptized, and receive the Holy Spirit. There were baptized then three thousand people (2:41), who "devoted themselves to the apostles' teaching and fellowship [*koinōnia*], to the breaking of bread and the prayers" (v. 42).

1. *All Things in Common* (2:42-47; 4:32-35). The first summary of community life (2:42-47) follows upon the mass baptism just mentioned (v. 41). On the level of the narrative, the influx of three thousand members into the community required some plan to meet the increased needs. The response was for the believers to

share voluntarily "all things in common." The term *koinōnia* in verse 42 refers to the common life, the fellowship and unity characteristic of the community. According to Luke this common fellowship was experienced by the sharing of possessions: "And all who believed were together and had all things in common [*koina*]; and they sold their property [*ktēmata*] and goods [*hyparchonta*] and distributed them to all, as any had need" (vv. 44–45). This summary statement assumes first of all that the believers owned property and other possessions. Their disposition was to put their private property at the disposal of the community by selling it and distributing the proceeds. The imperfect tense of the verbs "sell" (*epipraskon*) and "distribute" (*diemerizon*) suggests that the selling and distributing did not happen all at once but took place over a period of time whenever "any had need." Otherwise, the picture we have is that the property was maintained by the individuals or community until a need arose. Supporting this interpretation is that later in the narrative the community still had homes to gather in (5:42; 12:12).

The second summary passage about community life (4:32-35) is very similar to the first. The communal life is a visible and intrinsic dimension of the outpouring of the Holy Spirit (v. 31). Again, we hear that "as many as were possessors of lands or houses sold [*hypērchon,* imperfect tense] them" and that distribution "was made to each as any had need" (vv. 34, 35). Additional remarks by Luke give this community an ideal quality, fulfilling, on the one hand, the Greek ideal of friendship and, on the other hand, the Hebrew notion that there will be no needy person in the land. The Greek ideal is recalled with the expression "those who believed were of *one heart and soul*" (v. 32). There was a Hellenistic proverb before the time of Aristotle that "friends are one soul" and a saying attributed to Pythagoras that "friends hold all things in common."[3] Luke suggests that by sharing all things in common the community of believers realized this ideal. This community also realized a promise made in the Hebrew Scriptures: "There will be no poor among you" (Deut 15:4), since, as Luke comments, "There was not a needy person among them" (4:34). One further significant observation by Luke is

[3]See Johnson, *Sharing,* 119, for these citations.

that the proceeds from the liquidated property were laid "at the apostles' feet" (v. 35). This gesture, repeated in 4:35, 37; 5:2, means more than that the apostles were entrusted with the distribution of funds. It also symbolizes the submission of those who laid the proceeds at the apostles' feet to the authority of the apostles.[4] Within the overall plan of Luke-Acts, the twelve apostles assume from the religious leaders who rejected Jesus the prophet the authority over the renewed community of Israel.

Whether Luke in the two summary accounts of Acts 2:43-47 and 4:32-35 is describing the actual historical situation of the early Jerusalem community cannot be determined. Most commentators hold that these summaries originate with Luke and were not taken over from traditional sources. What Luke is expressing is that the sharing of material possessions is an outward manifestation of unity and caring within the community. Furthermore, placing one's possessions in common symbolizes the unanimity of mind and heart created by the outpouring of the Holy Spirit. For the Church of his own day, Luke used these ideal representations to say that property owners were to use their possessions for the benefit of the community, especially for those in need. Such action expresses unity in the fellowship and manifests the inner power of the Spirit.

2. *The Action of Barnabas* (4:36-37). Immediately after the second summary account Luke gives a concrete example of a person named Barnabas who disposes of his property. Barnabas sells a field (*agros*) he owns and brings the money to the feet of the apostles (4:36-37). Some commentators have suggested that his deed is out of the ordinary and for that reason it has survived in the tradition.[5] If so, then this lends support to the ideal portrayal of the early community by Luke in the summaries. In any case, Barnabas by his action demonstrates freedom from the bondage to his property. By giving the money to the apostles, he shows that he puts the needs of those in the community above preoccupations with holding on to personal possessions. Barnabas' posi-

---

[4]See Johnson, *Function*, 200–203, for this interpretation. Johnson bases this conclusion on the observation that one's disposition toward possessions symbolizes the disposition of the self.

[5]See, e.g., Ernst Haenchen, *The Acts of the Apostles* (Oxford: Blackwell, 1971) 233.

tive response stands in contrast, on the one hand, to the person in the Gospel parable who is too preoccupied with the field (*agros*) he has just bought to accept the banquet invitation (Luke 14:18) and, on the other hand, to the deceitful action of Ananias and Sapphira in the episode that follows in Acts.

3. *The Deceit of Ananias and Sapphira* (5:1-11). Like Barnabas, Ananias and Sapphira have sold a piece of property. However, after conspiring with his wife, Ananias has "kept back [*enosphisato*] some of the proceeds, and brought only a part and laid it at the apostles' feet" (5:2). As if God's providence were not enough, he keeps some of the money back as security.[6] Luke draws upon the story of Achan from the Hebrew Scriptures, who keeps back something for himself out of what is God's and for this reason is stoned to death by the community (Josh 7:1-26). On the face of it, the donation of even a part of the monies seems to be generous, but the problem is the deceit of Ananias and Sapphira. This conniving couple make themselves appear as if they are embodying the ideals of the fellowship of "one heart and soul," but instead their pretense violates trust and disrupts the Spirit-centered unity of the fellowship. Their sin is one of fraud. The consequences leave them imprisoned in their self-indulgence, and the communal harmony is undermined.

Peter has made it clear that they are perfectly free in their choices: to maintain possession of their property, to sell it, and if sold, to dispose of the proceeds as they see fit (v. 4). However, Satan tempts them and wins over their hearts. Luke believes that through the allurement of possessions, Satan can get control of one's decision-making capacity. The same has already happened to Judas, one of the Twelve. In the Gospel narrative, as the passion of Jesus draws near, "Satan entered into Judas" (Luke 22:3). Selling out to demonic power, Judas plots to betray Jesus for financial gain. By pledging himself "to the mammon of iniquity Judas has in fact concluded a pact with Satan himself.'"[7] With

6According to J. Duncan M. Derrett, "Ananias, Sapphira, and the Right of Property," *The Downside Review* 89 (1971) 225-232, it is not hard to see what this couple was up to. Derrett conjectures that Ananias kept back a sum of money to cover what is called his wife's *ketubah,* that is, the amount he must pay her if he divorced her unilaterally. Both Ananias and Sapphira plotted to keep some security for themselves in case the Church's system failed.

7Schuyler Brown, *Apostasy and Perseverance in the Theology of Luke.* AnBibl 38 (Rome: Pontifical Biblical Institute, 1969) 85.

the "reward of his wickedness" Judas goes out and purchases a field where he meets a violent death (Acts 1:18).[8] Similarly, Ananias and Sapphira are punished by a sudden death. All three of these people, Judas, Ananias, and Sapphira, are examples of the misuse of property. Each one succumbs to the temptation of Satan, who uses the enticement for material gain to separate them from the community and from God. Judas uses his ill-gotten gain to buy a field where he meets his death; Ananias and Sapphira deceitfully retain some of the proceeds from the sale of their property, leading to their deaths.

The implication of Judas' treachery is that the community of the original Twelve is diminished and hence the symbolic nature of this number loses its force, at least temporarily, until a replacement for Judas is chosen. The implication of Ananias and Sapphira's fraud is that the unity of the early community is broken. Together, these individuals serve as negative examples to those in Luke's Church who might be tempted by Satan to act for self-serving financial gain at the cost of the community.

4. *Neglected needs of the Greek widows* (6:1-6). The failure of Ananias and Sapphira to respond honestly and positively to life in the early community is no doubt a setback, but as Luke's narrative unfolds the apostles continue to work many "signs and wonders" (5:12) and "they did not cease teaching and preaching Jesus as the Christ" (5:42). Framed within two references to the increasing numbers of disciples (6:1, 7), Luke tells about another problem that arose. The Hellenists, who are probably Greek-speaking Jews from the Diaspora who have returned to Jerusalem to live, complain to "the Hebrews because their widows were neglected in the daily distribution" (6:1). The growing numbers and the diversity among the membership is presenting structural problems.

Luke does not explain why the widows of the Hellenists are neglected. Are the problems more than linguistic, including socioeconomic differences? Whatever the cause(s), the implication is that the "experiment" of love-motivated communism, which began after the Pentecost event, breaks down. Dissension arises

---

[8]Note that by taking on private ownership of property Judas was renouncing Jesus' call to his disciples to leave behind everything and follow him (5:11, 28; 18:22, 28).

within the community; no longer is it possible for the members
to say that they are "of one heart and soul" or that there is "not
a needy person among them" (4:32, 34).

To respond to the identified need, the community chooses seven
men with good reputations "full of the Spirit and of wisdom"
to be appointed (6:3). That all seven names are Greek indicates
that the group discriminated against is well represented by those
newly commissioned. Hence, they are in a position to understand
the interest of the oppressed and to respond with a commitment
strengthened by social and cultural ties with those they will serve.

The model offered here is worth reflecting on. Success in numbers and increased diversification among the members bring to
light the inadequacy of the current structural arrangements. Basic
needs of all the community members are no longer being met;
some are neglected. This calls for a creative response. The community then looks for individuals who first of all are "full of the
Spirit and of wisdom" and secondly, already have close ties with
the group to be served. The community is involved in the selection process. Then the candidates chosen are confirmed by the
laying on of hands by the apostles, those entrusted with authority over the community. This is one important model that Luke
proposed for the Church of his own day as a way to respond to
material needs that arose.

B. Almsgiving, Charity, and Community Offering

Individuals and communities are noted in the Acts narrative
for their good works and almsgiving to those in need.[9] First we
will look at a passage in which Peter and John seem to decline
a request for alms by a beggar. Then we will turn to two individuals known for their charity and almsgiving, Dorcas and Cornelius.
Finally, there are community-wide responses in the form of collections for other groups in need.

1. *A Crippled Man Begs for Alms* (3:1-10). Luke sets the stage
by describing the scene at the Temple where a man, lame from
birth, is brought on a daily basis to beg for alms (*eleēmosunē*)

---

[9]For a discussion of the organization of alms in the New Testament and other literature
see Robert M. Grant, *Early Christianity and Society* (London: Collins, 1977) 124–145.

from those entering the Temple (v. 3). When Peter and John walk by him on their way to the Temple, this lame man asks them for alms, with the expectation that he will receive something (vv. 4–5). Peter's response is "I have no silver or gold, but I give you what I have; in the name of Jesus Christ, walk" (v. 6). At that the man is healed and he begins praising God. By his reply Peter shows that he and John are being faithful to the mission charge given them in the Gospel narrative: "to heal" and to "take nothing for your journey, no staff, nor bag, nor bread, nor money" (Luke 9:2-3). No mention is made of the proceeds that the community has from the sale of their possessions (Acts 2:44-45). The apostles' encounter with the beggar at the Temple should in no sense be taken as a prohibition against almsgiving or material help for the poor and needy. What Peter offers is in fact far more than the man has requested; he is healed physically, which he demonstrates by "walking and leaping and praising God" (v. 8). Having been healed of his infirmity, the man is no longer among the outcast. Presumably, he will now be able to provide for himself the necessities of life.

2. *Tabitha, a Woman Known for Almsgiving* (9:36-43). There is at Joppa a Christian disciple (*mathētria*)[10] named Tabitha, which means Dorcas (a Greek word for "gazelle"). The fruits of her discipleship are notable: She is "full of good works [*erga agatha*] and acts of charity [*eleēmosunē*]" (v. 36). After Tabitha dies the disciples call for Peter, who comes to pray over her, and brings her back to life. Before Peter raises her up, the room where she lies is filled with widows who are "showing tunics and other garments," which Tabitha had made while she was with them. The assumption is that Tabitha supported these widows by her charity and that she had made the clothing that is being shown for them.[11] Hence, while the appointed seven men of the Spirit were handling the daily distribution for the Hellenistic widows in Jerusalem, Tabitha was supporting the widows in Joppa (modern Jaffa).

3. *Cornelius' Prayers and Alms are Remembered Before God* (10:1-48). Cornelius is a Roman centurion and a "God-fearer"

---

[10]This is the only example in the New Testament of the feminine *mathētria*.

[11]*See* Haenchen, *Acts*, 339.

(*phoboumenos ton theon*), known for his practice of giving alms (*eleēmosunē*) frequently to the people and for his continual prayers to God (v. 2). These were regular practices of his before the encounter with Peter and his subsequent baptism (vv. 47–48). Cornelius' almsgiving is a visible demonstration that his heart is not in bondage to his possessions but rather is open to the needs of others. His almsgiving, together with his prayers to God, suggests that he trusts in God rather than in himself or in his wealth.

In a vision of an angel from God, Cornelius is told, "Your prayers and your alms have ascended as a memorial before God [because of them God has remembered you]" (v. 4). Then Cornelius is instructed to send for Peter, who likewise has a vision. After Peter arrives, Cornelius reports to him the message that he has received from God during his vision: "Cornelius, your prayer has been heard and your alms have been remembered before God" (v. 31). After Cornelius testifies to his own religious experience of God, Peter confirms this: "Truly I perceive that God shows no partiality, but in every nation any one who fears him and does what is right is acceptable to him" (vv. 34–35). Then, after Peter instructs Cornelius about the good news of Jesus Christ (vv. 36–43), the Holy Spirit comes to all of them, and Cornelius, along with others who have heard, is baptized. Cornelius' sharing of his possessions and his prayers disposes him for the reception of God's messengers, both the angel and Peter, and prepares him for the outpouring of the Holy Spirit leading to baptism. Cornelius' religious practice before his baptism stands as an outstanding example for other Gentiles attracted to the Christian Way.

4. *The Disciples Give According to Their Ability* (11:27-30). Luke reports that during the days of Claudius a famine takes place so that relief is needed for the community of believers in Jerusalem. Prophets from Jerusalem are sent to Antioch to request material assistance to help alleviate the crisis. It is determined by the disciples in Antioch that "every one according to ability" (v. 29) should give to the relief fund (literally, "service, ministry," *diakonia*) for the mother Church in Jerusalem. The model for giving is somewhat different from that of the early community in Jerusalem, where all things are shared in common and the needs are met from this common fund. In Antioch the assump-

tion is that the believers retain their private property; they are asked individually to contribute according to their means.

Once the relief funds are collected, Barnabas and Saul take them to the Jerusalem Church. It is significant that in giving the Antiochian Christians are imitating the generosity of Barnabas, whose personal divestment for the sake of the community is undoubtedly known to them (cf. 4:36-37). By responding as they do, the believers from Antioch are expressing the unity between Gentiles and Jews within the Christian movement. Furthermore, they demonstrate their responsibility to alleviate suffering due to the lack of material supplies experienced by believers outside their own local community. Having transcended regional interest, they begin to embrace what today might be called a "global consciousness," and they respond accordingly.

5. *Paul Brings Alms and Offerings to Jerusalem* (24:10-21). We know from four of his letters (1 Cor 16:1-4; 2 Cor 1:16; 8–9; Gal 2:10; Rom 15:25-27) that Paul spent considerable effort organizing and taking up a collection for the Jerusalem Church.[12] Surprisingly, Luke is silent about Paul's endeavor until late in the Acts narrative. Before Felix the governor, Paul testifies that after some years he brought "to my nation" in Jerusalem "alms" (*eleēmosunē*) and "offerings" (*prosphora*) (24:17). This evidently was taken to the Temple (cf. v. 18). The assumption in Acts is that the collection Paul brings is for the Jews, whereas in the Pauline letters the collection is for the Christian community in Jerusalem. Luke tells nothing about who contributed to these "alms and offerings" nor about the spirit or motivation for the giving.

C. Misuse of Money to Subvert Religion

Just as the Gospel narrative identifies persons like the rich farmer and the rich man at the banquet table who are in bondage to their wealth and the comforts it affords, so also the Acts narrative brings to light persons who are enslaved by their money

---

[12]According to Paul in Gal 2:10, during his meeting with the Jerusalem leaders he was asked to "remember the poor." Paul lived up to this agreement by organizing the collection in several of his Churches.

and the power it has over them. Simon the magician offers the apostles money in exchange for the power to give others the Holy Spirit (8:9-24). Owners of a slave girl use her spirit of divination to bring them financial gain, that is, until Paul expels the spirit from her (16:16-24). In Ephesus there are many who practice magic, using expensive manuals said to be valued at fifty thousand silver pieces (19:18-20). Demetrius the silversmith has a thriving business making and selling silver shrines of the goddess Artemis (19:23-41). And Felix the governor, knowing that Paul has the collection with him, hopes that Paul will try to "buy him off" in order to earn his freedom (24:24-27). In each of these instances we have the actual or attempted misuse of money to subvert religious values and beliefs.

1. *Simon Offers Money for Spiritual Power* (8:9-24). Apparently a Samaritan, Simon is a practitioner of magic (*mageia*) (v. 9), who claims to be someone great (*mega*) (cf. 5:36).[13] Others, from the least to the greatest, are taken in by this claim, for they revere Simon as the embodiment of divine power: "This man is that power of God which is called Great" (v. 10). Over a period of time he amazes others with his magic (vv. 9, 11). However, when his devotees are evangelized and baptized by Philip, Simon himself is baptized. For Simon is impressed by the "signs and great miracles [*dynameis megalai*]" he has seen performed. The one who amazes others by his magical arts is himself amazed by the power of the living God. Perhaps because he has lost his clientele and his influence, Simon offers to purchase from the apostles Peter and John the power (*exousia*) to give the Holy Spirit to others. But Peter rebukes him: "Your silver perish with you, because you thought you could obtain the gift of God with money! You have neither part nor lot in this matter, for your heart is not right before God" (vv. 20–21). The power Simon wants to buy is a *gift* from God. He is to find out that spiritual benefits are not acquired by payment. Peter knows that Simon's heart is not right before God (v. 21; cf. Luke 9:47; 12:34), that he is "in the gall of bitterness and in the bond of iniquity [*syndesmon adikias*]"

---

[13]On this passage see J. Duncan M. Derrett, "Simon Magus (Acts 8:9-24)," *ZNW* 73 (1982) 52–68.

(v. 23).[14] These last two expressions are metaphors for the state of sin. Simon stands accused of idolatry (cf. Deut 29:17; 2 Kgs 9:22). After hearing Peter's words of judgment, Simon asks for his prayers (v. 25).

2. *Using a Slave Girl's Clairvoyant Spirit for Profit* (16:16-24). While in Philippi Paul and his companions meet a slave girl with soothsaying abilities. Her owners use her powers for their own financial gain. After Paul becomes sufficiently annoyed by her, he expels the spirit from her. At that the owners, whose vested financial interest is lost, seize Paul and Silas, drag them into the marketplace, where they bring a litany of accusations against them, none of which are the real reason for their anger against these two missionaries. As Charles Talbert astutely comments: "The economic motivation of those opposed to the Christian missionaries is masked behind various other appeals: Paul and Silas are branded as foreigners (an appeal to nationalistic feeling); they are labeled as Jews (an appeal to racial prejudice); they are described as purveyors of new ideas (an appeal to traditionalism); and they are depicted as opposed to Rome (an appeal to patriotism)."[15] The owners of the slave girl are not able to recognize how bound they are to the profit they gain through this girl's spirit of divination.[16] Also, the racket they have going leads their clients to rely upon knowing future events rather than to trust in God.

3. *The Burning of Valued Magical Books* (19:18-20). While in Ephesus Paul preaches and works extraordinary signs with the result that many become believers. Among these are practitioners of magic. Upon their conversion they confess and divulge their practices (v. 18). The narrator then records how their life has

[14]Note that in four of the six times that Luke uses the term "iniquity, unrighteousness" (*adikia*), it is used in connection with money: unjust steward (Luke 16:8), mammon of unrighteousness (Luke 16:9), Judas' reward of unrighteousness (Acts 1:18), and bond of unrighteousness (Acts 8:23). The other two instances are Luke 13:27 and 18:6.

[15]Charles H. Talbert, *Acts,* Knox Preaching Guides (Atlanta: John Knox, 1984) 70.

[16]The financial loss suffered by these owners has sometimes been compared to the herdsmen who lost their large herd of swine when Jesus sent the demons from a possessed man into swine, who then rushed down the bank and drowned in the lake (Luke 5:26-39). After this happened all the people asked Jesus to depart, for he had cost the people of the Gerasene countryside a financial loss. However, the main point of this Gospel story is not about a conflict between financial interest and religious interest but rather about the power of Jesus over demons.

changed, for they "brought their books [of magical arts] together and burned them in the sight of all; and they counted the value of them and found it came to fifty thousand pieces of silver" (v. 19). The value of these books is so great that this "detail" is remembered and thought to be worth recording in the narrative. The faith of the new believers is indeed genuine; they are willing to give up, even destroy, what is probably their most valued possession. As Robert O'Toole comments, "Given their nature, these books could not be sold and the money used for charitable purposes. Since the books would only lead their possible readers away from Jesus, they had to be destroyed in one way or another."[17] Neither the new converts nor the veteran apostle Paul is lured by the monetary value of the "treasure" before them. To sell the books rather than burn them would be to disregard the wider implications of such an action. Once the great monetary value of these books is renounced, the evangelical outcome is remarkable: "So the word of the Lord grew and prevailed mightily" (19:20).

4. *Demetrius the Silversmith* (19:23-41). The silversmith Demetrius has a thriving business, due in large part to the silver shrines he makes of the goddess Artemis. He and his fellow craftsmen soon come to realize that Paul's preaching has an adverse effect upon the sale of this product to the populace. Paul, they say, is telling the people "that gods made with hands are not gods" (v. 26). Demetrius voices a double concern to the craftsmen: that their trade will come into disrepute and that the goddess Artemis might even be deposed. This sparks a riot with two of Paul's companions, Gaius and Aristarchus, being dragged into the theater. This is a clear example of Christian monotheism posing a threat to the product line of a group of business people with a vested interest in the local cult. The religion Paul preaches cuts into their profits, and this causes a riot. Demetrius sees religion as legitimate only when it supports his economic enterprise and as dangerous when it threatens his vested interest.

5. *Felix Hopes for a Bribe from Paul* (24:24-27). During the time that he holds Paul as a prisoner, Felix the governor is evidently aware that Paul has just previously arrived in Jerusalem

---

[17]O'Toole, *Unity*, 134.

with the collection. For two years Felix keeps Paul imprisoned, during which time he frequently sends for Paul to have him speak about faith in Christ Jesus. But Felix has another, less honorable motive: "he hoped that money would be given him by Paul" (v. 26). This gives us two conflicting sides to Felix's intentions. According to the narrative, Felix may be genuinely interested in the Christian Way, but he also hopes for a lucrative bribe. Paul does become Felix's teacher, but he does not yield to his pressure to hand over any money. Hence, he remains in prison.

All of these people just discussed, Simon and the other magicians, Demetrius and his fellow silversmiths, the owner of the slave girl, and Felix are opponents of the apostles. They have in common the negative traits of greed and avarice. As such they share the same qualities as the opponents of Jesus in the Gospel. Thus in both the Gospel and Acts resistance to the good news is marked by those who are "lovers of money."

D. Hospitality

The Book of Acts continues and accentuates the Gospel theme of using one's possessions to offer hospitality. Jesus is frequently received as a guest, for example, by the Pharisees (7:35-50; 11:37-54; 14:1-24), Martha and Mary (10:38-42), and Zacchaeus (19:1-10). Often, as a guest, Jesus, through a role reversal, serves as host. He extends some manner of invitation to his hosts or table partners (see 5:29-39; 7:35-50; 10:38-42; 11:27-28; 14:1-24; 19:1-27; 24:13-35).[18] In this way the action of Jesus serves as an example. The believing community, especially the resident Church leaders, are to offer hospitality to others. Itinerant preachers who bring the gospel are to accept the hospitality from those who receive them, and in that context are to preach the good news (cf. 9:4-6; 10:5-9). As is true for the Gospel story of Jesus, in Acts hospitality offered to the missionaries is characteristically the context for extending peace and preaching the gospel.

In Acts hospitality is extended by evangelists, community members, new converts, God-fearers, and others. Among the evangelists, Aquila and Priscilla offer Paul a place to stay in Corinth

---

[18]See Koenig, *Hospitality*, 91.

(18:1-4), Philip opens his house to Paul in Caesarea (21:7-14), and Paul welcomes all who come to him while he lives in Rome under house arrest (28:30-31; see 28:16). From the community of believers, Judas gives shelter to Saul in Damascus after his "conversion" experience (9:11); Mary, the mother of John Mark, welcomes Peter into her home, where "many were gathered together and were praying" (12:12); Jason, at some risk to his own life, openly receives Paul, Silas, and other believers into his home at Thessalonica (17:5-9); and Mnason of Cyprus hosts Paul, his companions, and some disciples from Caesarea at his home in Jerusalem (21:16).

Frequently, those who have converted to the Way extend hospitality to the missionaries. The Gentile Cornelius receives Peter into his home at Caesarea and is baptized (10:24-48); the proconsul Sergius Paulus summons Paul and Barnabas to his place at Paphos in Cyprus to hear the word of God (13:7-12); Lydia, a business woman from Philippi, invites Paul to come to her house as a recognition of the sincerity of her belief: "If you have judged me to be faithful to the Lord, come to my house and stay" (16:15; cf. v. 40); and the jailer of Philippi brings Paul and Silas "up into his house, and set[s] food before them; and he rejoiced with all his household that he had believed in God" (16:34). In addition to these believers, the God-fearer Titius Justus hosts Paul in Corinth (18:7); Simon the tanner offers Peter a place to stay at his seaside home in Joppa (9:43; 10:6); and the inhabitants of Malta give Paul and his companions shelter from the cold and rain, showing them "unusual kindness" (28:2). Luke also comments that Publius, the chief man of the island of Malta, "received us and entertained us hospitably for three days" (28:7), during which time Paul heals Publius' ailing father.

Throughout the story of the early Christian movement, local Churches become banquet communities for itinerant missionaries, groups of believers, and probably nonbelievers as well. Many times those who hear the apostles preach believe, are baptized, and receive into their homes the bearers of the good news. In some instances the presence of the evangelists at the homes of these new converts signifies the validity of the faith received. Hospitality, offered and received, is an important way of establishing committed relationships in the faith between guests and hosts. Mutual welcoming leads to deeper levels of community and to greater inclusiveness. Koenig speaks about New Testament hospitality as a "partnership with strangers." He explains: "On the one hand, partnership with strangers signifies a joining of cobelievers, friends, and so on, in the expectation that new forms of reciprocity will take place among them. These in turn lead them to perceive their associates in a different light, perhaps as mediators of God's presence and therefore 'strange' in the best sense. On the other hand, partnership with strangers also suggests the forming of alliances with outsiders, foreigners, enemies, and so forth, in the conviction that God's redeeming work always discloses itself along these frontiers as well."[19] In both cases, partnership with cobelievers and partnership with outsiders, there is mutual giving, affirmation, and growth in the faith.

By using one's resources, whether these be homes, food, or money, to offer hospitality, basic needs are being met, but even more, the Christian community is being affirmed and extended. Bonds of solidarity are created between believers on a local level when community members gather in one home. When itinerant missionaries from other areas are received, covenantal ties are strengthened between regional Churches. And when evangelists accept the hospitality of new converts, the community grows beyond its own circles to embrace others who come to believe. Sharing of possessions by offering hospitality is an integral part of Luke's vision for the Church of his day.

Conclusion

At the beginning of his narrative about the early Church, Luke offers a way of handling possessions not encountered in the Gospel. In Luke's ideal portrayal, the Jerusalem community holds all things in common. They sell their property and distribute from the proceeds according to everyone's need, with the result that there are no poor among them. Possessions shared in common symbolize a unity among believers effected by the Spirit. This harmonious portrayal is soon shattered by the deceit of Ananias and Sapphira. Also, the neglected needs of the Greek widows call for

---

[19]*Ibid.*, 8-9.

an innovative change in the emerging institutional organization. Deacons with social and cultural ties to the oppressed are appointed to meet the material needs of these women. The reader of this development in Luke's narrative may well be prompted to reexamine existing contemporary Church structures and to initiate changes where they are inadequate in meeting community needs, both spiritual and material.

Besides the model of sharing all things in common, Luke presents two other ways of handling possessions from a faith perspective. One is almsgiving and the other is extending hospitality, both of which are important themes in the Gospel. Individual women and men are singled out for their generosity, Tabitha and Cornelius for almsgiving, Lydia and Paul for offering hospitality, to recall a few. Also, consistent with his apologetic concern, Luke shows how influential and well-off individuals are attracted to the Christian movement. Unlike some of the negative portrayals of rich people in the Gospel, these persons are not enslaved by their wealth. Instead they share it with others. Besides these individuals, whole communities of believers participate in a collection for another community in need. The contributions of the Antiochian Christians for the believers in Jerusalem is a clear example.

Luke also illustrates in Acts how money and the desire for accumulating it at any cost subverts religion. Simon's offer to purchase spiritual power (i.e., simony), Demetrius' selling of images of a pagan goddess, and Felix's hope for a bribe from Paul are all examples of ill-conceived projects by adversaries of the Gospel. Again, one may wonder to what extent similar problems were faced by the Lukan community.

At the end of this chapter it is fitting to point to one text from Acts not yet mentioned, and this is Paul's farewell address to the elders at Miletus (20:17-35). In this address Paul gives instructions to the local Church leaders from Ephesus whom he had summoned to Miletus. Presenting his own behavior as an example, Paul affirms: "I coveted no one's silver or gold or apparel" (v. 33). His motives in being a minister of the gospel are pure, not tainted with the desire for personal financial gain. The leaders of the Church Paul addresses are to shepherd the Church of God with no less integrity (cf. v. 28). Paul concludes this farewell address by recalling words of the Lord Jesus himself, " 'It is more blessed to give than to receive' " (v. 35). The Paul whom Luke portrays preserves this saying from the Lord, which is not found in any of the Gospels. This expresses well an underlying conviction to so much of what Luke says in his two-volume work about possessions and the Christian life. Perhaps it can stand as Luke's last word, too.

Conclusion

When a person begins to read the narrative of Luke-Acts, he or she expects to hear about "events that have been fulfilled" and "teachings" which have been received (Luke 1:1-4). When the reading of this story about Jesus and the early Church is finished, the reader can hardly miss the prominence of sayings and parables about possessions, those with them, those without, and the relations between these two groups. As we have seen, Luke not only takes over almost all of the material about these themes from his sources, Mark and Q, he also accentuates the demands found in the sources (e.g., leaving *all* or giving *all*) and adds to this tradition handed down to him much material about possessions, including such powerful parables as the rich person and Lazarus (16:19-31).

The prominence of economic matters in Luke's narrative makes it eminently clear that decisions about money and the use of a person's resources are indeed matters of faith. To compartmentalize questions of the economy, whether personal, institutional, national or global as purely secular matters, divorced from the concerns of the Gospel, is to innoculate oneself from the radical demands of the Gospel and the salvific perspective it offers. Unfortunately, believers too frequently keep their faith silent in money matters. The consequence is to risk not only one's own salvation, but the well-being of the community at large. A first response to the repeated question in Luke's narrative, "What ought we to do?" (Luke 3:10, 12, 14; 18:18; Acts 2:37) is to see one's faith in the God of Jesus Christ as a fundamental, indispensable perspective from which decisions are made in regard to economic questions. By bringing decisions about economics into the realm of faith, individual Christians and whole communities of believers can come to a deeper sense of integrity about their life before God.

In the dialogue between the contemporary reader and Luke-Acts, where might one's faith lead in dealing with the complex situation of economics as we approach the end of the twentieth century? Few are unaware of the global and national problems facing us, including the growing international debt, the unequal distribution of the means of subsistence, the Third-World poverty, the increasing gap between the rich and the poor in this country, the profit motif held as au ultimate value, the exploitation of human labor, and the national wealth being squandered on the proliferation of arms. Structures and social systems perpetuate such problems. On the personal level, many are faced with how to use the financial resources they have in a responsible way and to share these resources generously to meet human needs. What personal decisions are believers called to make so that global, national, and local economies can be redirected to meet the human needs of the many who are deprived of the prosperity enjoyed by the few? What is the primary action that God in Christ would have us take who are producers and consumers in today's marketplace?

While Luke does not give detailed answers for the complex economic questions facing us today, he does sketch various faith responses made with respect to possessions. In Luke's narrative some, like the men with a small fishing business on the Sea of Galilee, are called to renounce all their possessions, to become poor voluntarily in order to become disciples. Others are invited to give alms generously. Zacchaeus does this on his own initiative in response to the presence of Jesus who is a guest at his home. Another very frequent response to the reign of God is to offer hospitality, especially to those who are unable to reciprocate. More than once Jesus instructs those in his company to invite the poor, the sick, and the lame to their dinner table. Jesus himself frequently offers hospitality, as do many of the disciples in the Acts narrative. Also, in Acts, another model is to share all things in common and to use these resources to provide for the needs of the community members. Such sharing expresses and affirms unity in the fellowship of believers. Common to all these expressions of discipleship is the mandate not to cling to one's possessions and thus become their slave but to share them with others out of obediential faith in God.

Luke has a fair amount to say about the rich and the poor. Although the Lukan Jesus does not condemn the rich as such because of their wealth, nor does he glorify the condition of the poor, he does call the poor "blessed" and warns his listeners about the dangers of possessions. To use the image of a physician, Jesus diagnoses various symptoms of "mammon illness"[1] and offers healing to those so afflicted. Some run after material things and seek to find their life's security in the ever-greater accumulation of wealth. The rich farmer, isolated from the community, tries to find a sense of well being in this stored-up plenty. In others, this illness induces a state of numbness with regard to those around them. The rich man at the banquet table feels no compassion for poor Lazarus at his feet. More subtle is the symptom of split consciousness maintained by those who parcel their life into distinct spheres, serving mammon on the one side and attempting to serve God on the other.

A particular case of those afflicted with mammon illness is the literary portrayal of the Pharisees in the Gospel of Luke. The author labels the Pharisees, who are characteristically cast as opponents of Jesus and the disciples, as "lovers of money" (16:14), a typical description of opponents in Jewish and Greek literature of the time. Although the Pharisees claim to find favor with God because of their piety and religious deeds, they are portrayed as greedy and avaricious. Luke also evaluates their concern for purity laws as misguided and links this with their economic exploitation of others (see 11:39). Being aware of the various symptoms of mammon illness can be given as a second important response to the question in the Lukan narrative: "What are we to do?"

A third response to this question is to realize that Luke's narrative not only has relevance for individuals but also has implications for the social and economic relations of society as a whole. In other words, it calls for structural changes. For example, as

---

[1]This expression is used by Haughey, *Money,* 10.

Halvor Moxnes has pointed out,[2] Luke calls for a break in patron-client relationship. This means that those with resources are to give to others without the means of subsistence. Resources are to be shared without expecting any kind of reciprocity, whether this be a return of the favor, honor bestowed, or loyalty demonstrated. This is dramatically illustrated in the instruction about inviting those on the fringes of society, the destitute, to share in the "banquet" of life's necessity (Lk 14:12-14, 21-24; cf. 6:34-35), such that they and eventually all will have adequate food, drink, and shelter. Another example is the story of the poor widow (21:1-4). Placed within the context of Luke's narrative the words of Jesus in this story are a sharp criticism of a value system which takes economic advantage of the religious sensibilities of little people like the poor widow. These examples point to radical changes called for by the Lukan Jesus within societal relations.

For an economic system to be healthy a multitude of problems have to be solved, problems such as unemployment, hunger, homelessness, malnutrition, unequal distribution of resources, and the lack of basic health care. Responses to these community concerns can be made on at least two different perspectives. This can be done on the level of meeting an individual need, for example, helping a person to find a job, or a family to obtain housing. The response of many individuals or of a whole community sometimes has a cumulative effect bringing about a systemic change with the result that social institutions become more just and fair. A second way to respond to the deprivation many experience is to identify the injustices perpetuated by the existing matrix of social relations and to work, often through the political process, to transform these structures into more equable patterns of interaction.

A fourth response to the recurring Lukan question is, for the person of some means, to evaluate existing social and economic patterns from the perspective of the poor. Realistically, however, only those who through no choice of their own actually live in poverty day in and day out, year after year, generation after generation really know what the experience is like. It is families and communities like this who hear the words of Jesus in a way in which the comfortable of this world do not, in fact, cannot. A

----

[2]See above pp. 34-35.

persistent theme from the narrative of Luke is that the poor are the ones close to God, not the rich. By listening to the way the impoverished experience God, those who are well off may come to a new sense of liberation from the bondage brought about by the accumulation of possessions.

Beginning with the infancy narrative, it is the little people, those without status, power or privilege, who are the recipients of the glad tidings of the Savior's birth. The emperor, the governor, and the king also have their place in the story, not as those whose honor and esteem is enhanced in the eyes of their subjects, but rather as those who bring oppression and violence. In fact, as Mary proclaims in her hymn of liberation, the rulers are dethroned, the arrogant of mind and heart dispersed, and the rich sent away empty. Through a reversal of fortunes the lowly are lifted up and the hungry are filled with good things.

Later in the beatitudes the poor are called blessed not because of any virtue they might possess but simply because they are poor. To them Jesus says: "Yours is the kingdom of God." Already now they participate in God's reign, for they are in a privileged relationship with God. By calling the poor blessed, Jesus does not, of course, sanction the impoverished condition of those who are forced to live in that way. The reiterated calls to invite the poor into one's home and to give alms to the impoverished are indictments against the socially accepted practice of rendering the poor invisible and treating them as outcasts. Through the words and deeds of Jesus, their situation is reversed. The poor come to share in a wealth that the rich do not have.

For the contemporary Christian immersed in today's complex world, it is appropriate to take a metaphor from Paul the Apostle. That metaphor is that Christ may be my wealth (see Phil 3:8). There is an urgency that Christ be so named because of "the confusion that comes to all of us in our pursuit of things, and the hoping that the accumulation of monies is the wealth that will satisfy."[3] By making Christ one's wealth, personal faith speaks with a divine authority so that it can direct one's decisions about material and financial resources.

We began this book with an oft-repeated question from Luke's two-volume work: "What are we to do?" After having taken our

[3]Haughey, *Money*, 244.

own reflective journey with Luke through the Gospel and Acts, this query remains before us and calls forth from us with ever-greater urgency a faith response. To see all that we have as gifts to be shared rather than as things to be possessed is to strengthen bonds within the community of persons. To realize that who we are is more important than what we have is a significant first insight on the path to true freedom. What is at stake for us is nothing less than our wholeness and our salvation. What is at stake for the world is nothing less than the well being and wholeness of the entire human community.

Annotated Bibliography

Countryman, Louis William. *The Rich Christian in the Church of the Early Empire: Contradictions and Accommodations.* Texts and Studies in Religion 7. New York/Toronto: The Edwin Mellen Press, 1980. An informed study of early Christian attitudes toward wealth, its dangers and its benefits, in the first three centuries of the Common Era. The social context of these attitudes is explored, giving the reader valuable insights into the tensions within the Church. Includes helpful comments on Luke-Acts.

Degenhardt, H.-J. *Lukas Evangelist der Armen: Besitz und Besitzverzicht in den lukanischen Schriften.* Stuttgart: Katholisches Bibelwerk, 1965. Proposes that the disciples, who are to be equated with the officeholders in Luke's Church, are to renounce their possessions. The Pharisees are taken to be the opponents of Luke's community. These positions are rejected by most scholars.

Dupont, Jacques. "The Poor and Poverty in the Gospel and Acts." In *Gospel Poverty: Essays in Biblical Theology.* Chicago: Franciscan Herald, 1977. Dupont is particularly known for his monumental three-volume study, *Les beatitudes.* Louvain: Nauwelaerts, 1958, 1969, 1973.

Haughey, John C. *The Holy Use of Money.* New York: Doubleday, 1986. On the importance of one's life of faith in financial decision making. Includes a reading of Luke-Acts from a contemporary perspective. The author calls for a healthy economic anthropology wherein one's faith in the God of Jesus Christ informs the personal use of money and speaks to the transformation of the economic order so that it serves human needs.

Hengel, Martin. *Property and Riches in the Early Church.* Philadelphia: Fortress, 1974. A brief overview of property and riches, from the Old Testament to the early Church writers. The concluding ten theses help to bridge the gap separating us today from the early Church.

Johnson, Luke T. *Sharing Possessions: Mandate and Symbol of Faith.* Overtures to Biblical Theology 9. Philadelphia: Fortress, 1981. A provocative study about the symbolic function of possessions. One's attitude and use of possessions express the inner condition of the heart, one's faith in God, and one's love for fellow humans. All are called in some fashion to share possessions. This work is based on conclusions reached in the author's previous study, *The Literary Function of Possessions in Luke-Acts.* SBL diss. Series 39. Missoula: Scholars Press, 1977. The poor are the outcast among the people; the rich are those who have rejected the Messiah.

Karris, Robert. "Poor and Rich: The Lukan *Sitz-im-Leben.*" In Charles H. Talbert, ed., *Perspectives on Luke-Acts.* Perspectives in Religious Studies. Edinburgh: T & T Clark, 1978. Argues that although Luke's community had both rich and poor members, Luke was primarily taken up with the rich, their problems, and their concerns.

Keck, Leander E. "The Poor Among the Saints in the New Testament." *Zeitschrift für Neuentestamentliche Wissenschaft* 56 (1965) 100–129. Author discusses the summaries of the early community and the collection of Paul in Acts. The "poor" in the Gospel refers to the actual condition of the Church.

Koenig, John. *New Testament Hospitality: Partnership with Strangers as Promise and Mission.* Overtures to Biblical Theology 17. Philadelphia: Fortress, 1985. A stimulating reflection on the dynamics of hospitality and the establishment of committed relationships between guests and hosts. Argues that Luke writes primarily for resident community members and their obligations toward nonbelieving neighbors and wandering charismatics.

Malina, Bruce. "Wealth and Poverty in the Early Church." *Interpretation* 41 (1987) 354–367. *Idem.,* "Interpreting the Bible with Anthropology: The Case of the Poor and the Rich." *Listening* 21 (1986) 148–159. Focuses on the distinctive connotations of wealth and poverty in the New Testament, approached from a cultural-anthropological perspective. Placed in their cultural context of the New Testament, the terms "rich" or "wealthy" generally meant "avaricious" and "greedy," while "poor" referred to the socially impotent, those who could hardly maintain their honor or dignity.

Mealand, David L. *Poverty and Expectation in the Gospels.* London: SPCK, 1980. Traces the traditions from the time of Jesus to that of Luke. Asserts that Luke did not accentuate the hostility toward riches that came to him form his sources. Luke gives advice to the rich as to how to use their wealth generously and to warn them of its dangers.

Moxnes, Halvor. *The Economy of the Kingdom. Social Conflict and Economic Relations in Luke's Gospel.* Philadelphia: Fortress, 1988. A clear and astute application of social science methods to the Lukan narrative. Moxnes explains well the dynamics of patient-client relations and contrasts to this the "moral economy of the peasant" offered by Luke. There are also fresh insights on the role of the Pharisees within the narrative.

Neyrey, Jerome H. (ed.). *The Social World of Luke-Acts. Models for Interpretation.* Peabody, Mass.: Hendrickson, 1991. This wide-ranging collection of articles provides very helpful cultural-anthropological windows for viewing the social world of Luke. Topics covered include: honor and shame, the pre-industrial city, the countryside, sickness and healing, patron-client relations, and the symbolic universe of Luke-Acts.

Pilgrim, Walter. *Good News to the Poor.* Minneapolis: Augsburg, 1981. An instructive study of the material on the poor and possessions in Luke-Acts. The author discusses the poor at the time of Jesus, Luke's use of traditional material in the Gospel, and Luke's perspectives. Whether or not one is fulfilling the mission of Jesus to the poor is directly related to one's attitude toward possessions.

Schottroff, Luise, and Wolfgang Stegemann. *Jesus and the Hope of the Poor.* A soundly based academic study written from a sociological perspective, which attempts to discern the social setting of the historical Jesus movement, of the people behind the sayings source, and finally of the Lukan community.

Seccombe, David Peter. *Possessions and the Poor in Luke-Acts.* Studien zum Neuen Testament und Seiner Umwelt. Series B, Vol. 6. Linz: 1982. A dissertation that maintains that a consistent, unified vision controls the hand of Luke. The author equates the "poor" with the whole nation of Israel in need of God's salvation, and the rich with Gentile oppressors of Israel. Luke writes for the well-to-do Hellenistic God-fearers, who had much to lose if they became Christian.

Stegemann, W. *The Gospel and the Poor.* Philadelphia: Fortress, 1984. This little book offers a vivid picture of the poor at the time of Jesus, portrays the social status of groups of Christians in the early Church, and concludes with reflections for affluent Christians today.

U.S. Bishops' pastoral message and letter, "Economic Justice for All: Catholic Social Teaching and the U.S. Economy." *Origins,* vol. 16, no. 24 (November 27, 1986) 410–455. A widely acclaimed statement about the moral dimensions of economic decisions. Chapter 2 includes a section on biblical perspectives.